WHEN I GROW UP

I WANT TO BE . . .

....

THE MEMOIR OF GINO NARBONI,
AS TOLD TO
CHARLOTTE NARBONI

THIRD EDITION

To Jamie
with admiration
for your many strengths
Charlotte

SAN ANTONIO, TEXAS

January 2019.

Charlotte Narboni
http://www.whenigrowupginonarboni.com

Front Cover: Gino Narboni, Constantine, Algeria 1925,
Back Cover: Gino Narboni, 90 years, 2013, Marcy Maloy, Photographer

WHEN I GROW UP I WANT TO BE . . . Third Edition
1st Edition Print   October 2013 ISBN 978-0-615-88548-3
2nd Edition eBook – March 2014 eISBN 978-0-9860728-0-2
2nd Edition Print – July 2014 ISBN 978-0-9860728-1-9
3rd Edition Print - April 2017 ISBN 978-0-9860728-2-6
3rd Edition eBook – April 2017 eISBN 978-0-9860728-3-3

To Charlotte,
Life restarts when you enter the room.

And to my darling daughters, Nicole and Cecile,
Your unconditional love is the greatest gift I have ever
received.

Travaillez, prenez de la peine,
c'est le font qui manque le moins.

–LA FONTAINE

Work hard, be unstinting in your efforts, because that
(hard work and effort) is the fund which is the least
lacking

TABLE OF CONTENTS

....

PREFACE

For years, when friends and acquaintances have asked about my history and I have recounted the circuitous journey that has taken me from North Africa to France and finally to America, they always say, "You should write a book." That's easier said than done. In spite of my family's encouragement, and even nagging, (Charlotte's words, not mine) I just never got around to it. Maybe because I think I haven't done anything particularly remarkable and no one would want to read about my travels through life.

Five years ago, after the last significant birthday observance, Charlotte bought a tape recorder and wrote down a series of questions for me to answer. I sat alone in my office, trying to recount just one phase of my life. It wasn't much fun. However, I dutifully filled one cassette tape. After we had transcribed and read my musings, we looked at each other and agreed to return to it at a later date. That date is now here. I am about to turn 90, and with the help of my family I will finally tell my story.

However, I must give credit where credit is due. We would not even be at this part in the process if it had not been for a couple we met during our 2012 Seabourn *Quest* Caribbean cruise. This ship carries about 400 passengers and because it's small we have an opportunity to meet most of the other guests. The warm air, blue seas, and bright sunlight make it easy to sit in one of the outdoor restaurants and strike up a conversation with folks at a neighboring table. Let's be honest. It's Charlotte who 9 times out of 10 starts the ball rolling, but we often meet other passengers who can keep up the verbal momentum. The conversation begins, the guests hear my accent and my Italian-sounding name, and when I announce that I am French the questions start coming.

With my advancing years, I find it harder to talk in public, particularly about my life story. I confess I often skip over events and abbreviate sections. Sometimes I forget or can't be bothered to go into details. Fortunately, I always have Charlotte at my side and you know Charlotte; nothing is left unsaid. Any detail I attempt to omit is highlighted and I am encouraged to reinsert it. Finally, if Charlotte becomes too frustrated with the slow pace, she just takes over the story. Does that surprise you?

This sequence of events has happened so often that Charlotte and I have developed an unstated plan of action for telling the story. I begin and if the listeners appear interested, with Charlotte's help, we recount the different stages of my life and make it into a long-running serial. At some time in the history telling, we announce we'll share more at a later time. This releases them from hearing further details of my peregrinations if they have more compelling projects lined up.

One fine morning, we found ourselves sitting next to a Swedish couple. At some point, after exchanging pleasantries, the question of my background arose. We started with the abbreviated version since we had finished breakfast and it was time to get on with the day's activities, but we made a date to continue the story the next day.

At the time, I did not know their last name. We learned, however, they lived on the island of Tortola in the British Virgin Islands but spent four months during the summer at their house in Sweden. When we finished my storytelling, to reassure me it could be done, Bengt confided that he had written a book about his career and life with Birgitta.

Today, with the resources of the Internet, self-publishing has lost its vanity press stigma (look at YouTube's success). If you think about it, telling your life story for your friends and family can be a vital oral history written down. We didn't know what Bengt and Birgitta's working life had been about or how they had ended up in Tortola, other than not wanting to shovel snow in northern Sweden. We exchanged cards as we said our goodbyes.

Two days after we returned home, a package arrived from Tortola. In it was a copy of a book with a cover photo of Bengt as a young man, holding a large bouquet of flowers. We were intrigued by the title: *A Entrepreneurial Life: The Story of the Delivery Boy who became the Flower King of Sweden.* When we finished reading Bengt's memoir, Charlotte and I knew the time had come to tell my story.

So, please let me say thank you to Bengt and Birgitta Nygren for starting us on this path of remembrance.

PREFACE
SECOND EDITION

....

Charlotte and I are grateful for the many kind words we received following the publication of WHEN I GROW UP, I WANT TO BE . . .

Here we are one year from the time we first began putting the story of my life on paper. We realize many potential readers prefer to read electronically, so we have prepared this second edition.

One learns quickly that in spite of multiple readings, endless fact checking, more readings, and additional investigation, print and fact gremlins are always lurking nearby, with some avoiding capture at all costs. The first edition of my memoir did not escape the assault of these literary bad boys. We have taken steps to correct some dates, misspellings, and even a factual error or two.

Most importantly, thanks to our cousins, we have been able to enhance and broaden some of the family sto

PREFACE
THIRD EDITION

....

The final chapter had to be written. My darling husband, Gino Narboni, left us last summer. His final months, filled with the love of his family and friends, provided a suitable ending for a life well lived.

Although this third and final edition to *When I Grow Up, I want To Be, . . . The memoir of Gino Narboni as told to Charlotte Narboni*, was written without Gino's participation, his thoughts and beliefs were in my thoughts as I wrote.

Let me say thank you one more time to all of our family and friends, some who were identified in the memoir and many others who were not mentioned. I know Gino would join me in appreciation for your friendship and loyalty.

ACKNOWLEDGEMENTS

....

It is not an exaggeration to say that writing this memoir would have been impossible without the assistance of friends, some of whom we've known for many years and others whose paths we have crossed more recently.

This has been a group project. First, let me give credit to Gino Narboni whose remarkable life story provided the inspiration for putting the words on paper. Our dear daughters, Nicole and Cecile, provided stories, long since forgotten by Gino and me. "Are you going to write about?" and off I'd go, adding more pages to the manuscript. Many of these passages would not have made it into the book without their input. I hope it is richer for their inclusion. As critics, our daughters never hesitated to set me on the right path if I strayed too far from either grammar or literary norms. You have to be from my generation to appreciate the joy of commas. Any overuse is my mistake, not that of Nicole or Cecile.

Charles Clark, our friend from Austin, never stopped taking my phone calls in spite of comments from his other friends. "Aren't you done helping that woman yet?" Many afternoons, too numerous to count, we'd spend hours removing excess commas, cleaning up gross grammatical errors, and even rewriting sections so Gino's story made sense to those who are reading it for the first time.

No one can sort through complicated regulations and overcome technical hurdles better than our friend Nickey McCasland. In helping us put this book together, he provided the tools to work through the copyright process. Nickey is also responsible for making the Official 90th Birthday Celebration Web site a reality.

I had the counsel of a completely bilingual, professional writer. Paris-based Bernard Edinger, who had been a Reuters reporter during his working life, is one of those fortunate individuals who can think, speak, write, and I imagine dream, in English and French without error or accent. Early in the process, he offered to read the manuscript as it was being written. In addition to providing e-mail encouragement, often on a daily basis, Bernard corrected historical inaccuracies and added his perspective on military life and conflict in the 20th century. Any errors are mine.

We met Dr. Karen Brooks, a novelist from Tasmania, during a cruise along the Turkish coast last year. She's a shining example of beauty and brains and, by the way, she has a killer sense of humor. Karen read my manuscript, again via e-mail, as I wrote, and since she said she loved it, Karen will always be my friend.

This was a hands across the sea project, thanks to the modern wonders of e-mail and digital scans. I had assistance from Patrice Laverdet, who lives near Paris. Patrice wanted to keep alive the memory of his grandfather (also a French Army Air Force pilot in the U.S. flight program) and has collected photos and historical data about this era. Thanks to Patrice's work, Les Centres de Formation du Personnel Navigant en Amérique, we learned much more than Gino could remember about actual dates for his own progression through the U.S. flight school program during WWII.

Julia Daninos, a cousin and granddaughter of *Opera Comique* tenor Lucien Daninos, nephew Pascal Narboni and our cousins Guy Castel and Dolly Narboni, also provided photos and information about the family.

For information about the Jewish migration into Livorno, Geoff DeVito, a travel anthropologist, led us to Dr. Gabriele Bedarida. As the archivist for the Synagogue Ebraica in Livorno, Dr. Bedarida confirmed that several family names were indeed listed in the Synagogue records.

Thank you to all who have helped us tell Gino's story. We think it's a good one.

—Charlotte Narboni

ONE

FAMILY HISTORY

lgeria seems a world away from my current Texas home. In spite of the headlines that dominate the coverage of events in the Middle East and North Africa today, most Americans still can't picture life in this region. Yet, the first 18 years of my life were spent in Constantine, Algeria, a medium size city about 200 miles from the capital, Algiers.

My story begins with the French invasion and conquest of Algeria in the 1830s. From that period until 1962, this country was considered part of France. Unlike its neighbors, Morocco and Tunisia, which were French Protectorates, Algeria was completely French. The school system, the money, the banks, and the legal administration were under the control of France. The relationship between the French living in Algeria and their counterparts in the homeland was close and special. Think of Americans who live in Alaska or Hawaii today.

These states don't share borders with other states, but the citizens of these areas are 100 percent American!

Our family names, Narboni, Aboucaya, Kouia, Namia, Daninos, and Bacri don't sound Jewish, do they? All are Sephardic, but unlike their Eastern European cousins, the Ashkenazi, the history of the Sephardic Jews began in North Africa. As wandering Jews, they took a different path into Europe, following the Moors into Spain in the early part of the eighth century. Like the Moors, the Jews remained on the Iberian Peninsula until the 15th century.

There is documentation the Narboni name first surfaced in the southern French town of Perpignan during the early 1300s. Records indicate Moses Narboni, a philosopher and physician, was born there, but at some time in his life he moved to Spain, settling first in Toledo and later in Barcelona. His writings include more than 20 essays as well as commentaries and treatises on philosophy, Judaism and the meaning of the Torah.

The next Sephardic migration occurred in the 15th century. The Jews followed the Christians as they continued to retake Spanish territory from the Moors. The last of the Muslims were pushed out of the Spanish peninsula in 1492, during the reign of Ferdinand and Isabella. This was also the time of the Inquisition, created earlier to rid Spain of non-believers. The Inquisition forced all non-Catholics, including Jews and Muslims, to

convert. If they refused, they were tortured and executed. The Inquisition ended with the final exodus of the
Moors, but the policy had forced most Jews out of the
region by the turn of the 16th century.

The Jews began their return towards North Africa.
Some, including my ancestors, moved first to neighboring European countries. Livorno, a port city on the western coast of Italy, became an active settlement for
Sephardic migration. From there, members of our family, including the first Narboni's began sailing to Algeria
in the mid-1700s, and along with other relatives, some
close and some distant, followed the sea path across the
Mediterranean to Algeria and Tunisia. They were already
settled in North Africa when the French king, Charles X
began his invasion in 1830. One of the stated reasons for
the French invasion was to rid the area of the Barbary
pirates, but a closer look at history reveals an ugly period
of conquest by the French against the native Muslims
and an attempt to defeat the Ottomans, who controlled
that area.

Although our North African history starts in Algeria,
family names also crop up in Tunisia and Egypt. According to family documents, David Narboni, our patriarch,
who married Anna Kouia, was born in Livorno, Italy
around 1780. It is not established when he sailed for Algiers, but our records show he and his family lived at 10
rue Pompeii, in that city.

One of their three sons was my great-great grandfather Salomon, born in Algiers between 1800-1830. He moved to Constantine in 1877, eventually becoming *Conseillier-Général* (a government official). His wife, Lonna Aboucaya, was also born in Algiers. After they married, they moved to Setif, a town in northeastern Algeria. Their four children included my great-grandfather, David Narboni. He was a leader in the Jewish community, a member of the Municipal Committee, the General Counsel and President of the *Consistoire*, the religious governing body that regulated the lives of Jews in Algeria. My paternal great-grandparents, David and Anna Narboni, née Aboucaya, had five children, including a son, Nathan. My paternal grandfather, Nathan Narboni, for whom I am named, was born in Setif in 1861 and died in 1905 when my father was 13 years old. His wife, my grandmother, Anna Aboucaya, had passed away in 1897 at an even younger age, leaving my father and his brother and sister to be raised by his Uncle Elie Narboni.

You have every right to be confused about this condensed description of my family history; I am, as well. I do know that Fortunée, my maternal grandmother, an Aboucaya, born and raised in Setif, married Victor Emmanuel Daninos and moved to Tunisia after their marriage. Their daughter, Aurette, who was born in Sousse, Tunisia, married Georges, Nathan's son. Edith, the eldest of Fortunée's five daughters, married David Narboni, also one of Nathan's sons. This meant both Aurette and Edith married their first cousins, Georges and David. I am the son of Georges and Aurette. No wonder Charlotte says I looked outside the family for new blood.

Although my mother and father were first cousins, they were born and raised in different countries. They met after Edith and David were married and Edith moved from the family home in Sousse, Tunisia to Constantine, Algeria.

Now that we have begun writing this story of my life, we have learned through our research that Jewish families in this era often married cousins. As Jews, most likely observant, they lived in close quarters, which you may or may not want to call ghettos. Certainly, their homes were in an enclave.

This close living may not have been necessary, since in a fairly remarkable gesture, given the history of anti-Semitism throughout the centuries in both Europe and the Middle East, French Jews who settled in Algeria were granted full citizenship about 40 years after the initial invasion. The 1870 document that made this possible, the *Décret Crémieux*, was written by Adolphe Crémieux, a French politician. The Décret Crémieux remained in effect until the fall of France in 1940, following the takeover of Algeria by the German-controlled Vichy French government.

My father, Georges, who was born in 1892, began medical studies in Paris in 1912. When World War I started in 1914, Georges was drafted as a stretcher-bearer, but shortly after his induction into the army, he received an officer's commission. Since he had some professional medical training, he was placed in charge of a field first-aid station.

Once it became clear the conflict was not going to end quickly, a belief held by all sides at the beginning of the war, trenches were built along the front lines, mostly in the French countryside. Basically, the trenches were used to "dig in" to a position and to avoid losing ground. Although the use of trenches had been known since ancient times, they were developed more fully during WWI. To protect their forces, both sides created underground passages in sections of varying lengths, from eight to 20 feet, and depths up to 10 feet. The trenches were dug along long swaths of territory, from Switzerland's border with France to Belgium in the North.

Accounts of life in the trenches are nothing short of horrific. Trench warfare became the primary launching platform for battle advances and retreats. The fighting above ground was often fierce and deadly. Even if a soldier survived the assaults when they "went over the top" the secondary problems of living in the trenches created serious health conditions. Trench foot, lice, and dysentery were common complaints. Eventually, those who lived through the front-line battles rotated to the trenches and then to encampments towards the rear before restarting the cycle again.

My father followed the same rotation schedule. As the head of a first aid unit, he was assigned to the Ardennes forest region of St. Menehould, a town in eastern France. In the early stages of the war, Georges was injured and hospitalized for a head wound from flying shrapnel. After his recovery he returned to the front lines, but in 1916 my father was wounded again, seriously this time. He and his men were ordered to establish a medical clinic in a village church, but before setting up their station, the soldiers inspected the site. When they descended into the church basement they walked into pockets of mustard gas trapped below the main floor. Realizing their predicament, the men rushed to get out. Georges, who was one of the lucky ones, told us he survived because as an officer he was among the first to be evacuated.

My father was blinded and hospitalized with multiple injuries from the gas inhalation. After his sight returned, he was declared fit for limited duty. For the remainder of the war, he was assigned to a hospital in Constantine, Algeria that cared for severely wounded soldiers, who like he, would not be returning to the front. There, he told us he made daily hospital rounds on his horse, Lily. Finally, in 1918, after four years of terrible fighting, the war ended and an Armistice was signed. My father was fortunate. He survived.

However, the effects of the mustard gas poisoning, including chronic bronchitis and corneal scarring of his eyes, remained a serious health problem for the remainder of Georges' life. In the '30's, nearly two decades after he was wounded, my father was fitted with scleral lenses. Although these thick glass lenses, which cover most of the eye's surface, protected his damaged corneas, they gave his eyes an unnatural glassy look.

Georges' bravery was recognized with two important citations. He was awarded the Chevalier de la Légion d'Honneur, pour faits de guerre. The French Legion of Honor medal, created by Napoleon Bonaparte, is given for service to the State. This can be for any notable achievement, but Georges received his medal for bravery during combat. Later in his life, my father was promoted to Officier de la Légion d'Honneur. Georges also received the Croix de Guerre, with one palm and three stars. The combination award meant he earned it four times over, i.e. like an oak leaf cluster on U.S. medals. The "palm" decoration signified he was given the honor à l'ordre de l'armée, the highest Croix de Guerre possible, an award rarely bestowed.

Georges went to Paris in 1918. After completing both his medical studies and advanced training in obstetrics and gynecology, in 1920 he returned to Constantine. In spite of his precarious health, my father worked hard every day, retiring only as he and my mother left Algeria in 1964.

Georges and my mother, Aurette Daninos, were married in 1922. Aurette, whose given name was Aure-Alix, was one of eight children, six of whom survived into adulthood. She was born in Sousse, Tunisia, but moved to Constantine, Algeria after her marriage to my father.

The Daninos sisters lived in an era and area where few women received an education beyond high school. Mother was no exception. Before her marriage, her father warned my mother, "You will be a nurse all your life if you marry Georges." This warning turned out to be true, as my father, 13 years older than Aurette, had chronic health problems associated with his war wounds.

TWO

....

LIFE IN CONSTANTINE

Mother was 18 years old at the time of my birth. Mario, my brother, arrived 13 months later and Yvan, my youngest brother, was born in 1927. Aurette had her hands full! Three boys in the space of four years and their attendant needs took all of my mother's time. It was much later in my life I realized the difficulties my mother had faced. Although she had household help, including an Italian nanny for my brothers and me, Aurette was still responsible for our growth and education. Caring for my father added to her workload.

There's no other way of saying it: We were bad boys. As the ringleader, I enlisted Yvan and our cousin Claude Narboni for our escapades. The three of us worked together to torment Mario. Although such behavior was forbidden, we seldom hesitated to break the rules. Nor were we allowed to leave our garden but we frequently ignored that prohibition and snuck out. Inevitably, we were caught and punished. Corporal punishment was a fact of life for the Narboni *frères*.

In the early years of our childhood, we lived in an apartment on the floor above my father's office. I still remember the building address: 6 Rue Caraman, a street in the center of Constantine. My father, who was 30 years old when he married, had a difficult life. Nothing was easy for him. The war, the interrupted medical training, his marriage to a girl still in her teens and three children left little time for entertainment. Underneath the problems mentioned, I suspect the lingering side effects from the mustard gas poisoning kept him from ever really feeling strong or fit. His responsibilities and burdens must have weighed heavily on him.

Georges workday was full. He saw his patients, mostly Arab women, at the office and in the hospital, where he was Chief of Obstetrics. My father, revered and respected in the Muslim community, was addressed as *Toubib*, the Arabic word for doctor.

As Algerian had large families, any woman unable to bear children would be sent to a physician, even a Jewish one, to seek help. Georges routinely performed D & C's in his office. This procedure, in which the interior lining of the uterus is scraped, was done without anesthesia. Georges would caution the patients that there might be some pain. The women seemed unfazed by the notion of discomfort. One woman told him to worry about the surgery; she would worry about the pain.

My father never mentioned any prohibition against seeing female patients without an additional female in the examining room. I take this as a practical fact of life; the patients were there for assistance in their pregnancy or to seek help if they could not conceive. Any late-20th century rules did not apply in this part of the world.

Since my father's eyesight was limited, I was pressed into service as an extra pair of eyes when he went out to deliver a baby after dark. As the oldest, I sat in the front seat next to my father to warn him if an obstacle appeared in the road. Once we arrived at the house, I'd curl up in the back seat, covered with a blanket. I'd hear the woman wailing while I waited for my father's return after the delivery. Then, I would guide him as he drove back to our house. On one of these nighttime trips, a man suddenly appeared in front of our car. I don't know why I didn't warn him, but my father did not see him and knocked him to the ground. We drove the man to the hospital; fortunately, his only injury was a broken arm, which was set before he was released.

Our lives, as I mentioned, revolved around school and our family. Most of our traveling involved visits to other family members, usually to see my mother's relatives in Tunisia. Occasionally, during the summer months, we drove to the beach at Phillippeville, a town on the Mediterranean Sea just 50 miles from Constantine.

For some reason, unknown to me, my father loved cars, a trait I have inherited. We had a Hotchkiss, circa 1935, and before that a Citroën. The Hotchkiss, with its leather side panels in the doors, was considered a luxury car. My mother also drove, so we became a two-car family when my parents bought a Matford (combination Ford and Mathis) and a Ford.

No one seems to know or have any idea about what life in Algeria is like. If you keep up with the news today, Algeria makes news, but as with all the other times the country has been on the news since 1962, the headlines are never good.

Algeria is nearly four times the size of Texas. The country stretches from the Mediterranean on the northern border to the vast Sahara Desert on the south. Foreigners may know about Algeria because of its vast oilfields, but they seldom have any knowledge about its mountains, the deep gorges that drop from the high ranges, the great Sahara desert, or even the beautiful prehistoric cave paintings in southeast Algeria, now protected as a World Heritage site.

The country is incredibly rich in mineral wealth. The mining of minerals, including phosphates, is exceedingly important as an export worldwide. Surprisingly, there are four seasons in parts of Algeria. Constantine, in the northern half of the country is 4,000 feet above sea level so it was not unusual for us to see snow in the winter. The city, built on a precipice, overlooks a gorge 300 feet below. A suspension bridge, Sidi M'Cid, completed in 1912, was for 17 years, the highest structure of its kind in the world.

In the early '30s, we sold the apartment and office building on Rue Caraman and moved to Sidi Mabrouk, a predominately Jewish neighborhood in a Constantine suburb. Sidi means sir and *mabrouk* is the Arabic name for good luck.

There, we bought a large two-story house from its Italian architect/builder. The living area, dining room and kitchen were on the *rez de chausée* or ground floor. The bedrooms and bathroom were on the second floor, which for the French is the first floor. Georges and Aurette lived in this house until 1964, when they moved to Paris following Algeria's independence from France.

In recalling our life in Algeria during the 1930s for this memoir, I am struck by how little daily life has changed since that time. Remember, we lived in North Africa . . . not exactly Middle America!

Although I call it a suburb, Sidi Mabrouk was really in the country. To go into Constantine, we took a city bus on the Sidi Mabrouk line.

Even though we lived in a predominately Muslim country, we felt safe and reminded ourselves that as

Jews, unlike those in so many other parts of the world, we were under the protection of the Décret Crémieux, the law that granted us the right of full French citizenship.

That sense of security was broken on August 5, 1934, when riots broke out in Constantine. I was 11 at the time. Most of the violence occurred in the old Jewish quarter. Jews had lived next to Arabs in Algeria for centuries and although there were occasional disputes, for the most part, it was a peaceful co-existence. This time, however, was different. It was a one-day pogrom with serious consequences. We were not affected since my father was known in the Arab community. But, in the interest of safety, we stayed inside our house in Sidi Mabrouk and kept the doors and windows locked. The day, which passed without any police or army protection, left 27 dead, including 25 Jews; among that number: five children, six women and 14 men.

Apart from this one violent upheaval, my brothers and I lived an ordinary, somewhat dull life. We went to the movies on Saturday. On Sundays, our family would drive with my cousin Claude and his sister, Nicole, and their parents, David and Edith, into the countryside for picnics. You may remember from an earlier chapter that David and Georges were brothers and Aurette and Edith were sisters.

I attended our French public school until I was 18. It was located at the edge of the cliff overlooking the gorge. Ali, the gardener's son, drove us to school and picked us up at the end of the day. If Ali was not available, we walked to my father's office and waited for him until it was time to go home. Remembering this life makes me think our life was not that much different from a middle class family in a European or American environment.

Most of us have stories about our parents' crazy ideas. We were no exception. My father believed that not wearing socks made one healthier, so we went to school, even in the winter, in sandals.

I don't remember much about school, but it wasn't fun. There weren't any electives. School is school. It's hard or easy, depending on your abilities. I was good in English and French, but not that proficient in science and mathematics. When we returned from school, after we had our *gouter,* or snack, we went straight to our homework. My mother was a severe taskmaster. Heaven help us if we brought bad grades home.

Food was an important part of our lives. We didn't think about it; we just accepted that we ate well. Aurette was an excellent cook. As I mentioned, my mother had help in the kitchen, but she prepared most of the meals. Breakfast was simple: bread and butter with café au lait. Mother made coffee for my father with the first "pressing." Our coffee came from pouring the water through the grounds a second time.

One of my jobs was to pick up milk from our Arab neighbors. I carried a milk container from home, knocked on the farmhouse door and turned my back before it opened. A young woman, probably without her head covered, took the bottles, filled them, set them outside, and shut the door. Only then could I turn around.

Just like students today, we either carried our lunch or ate in the school cafeteria. Although we had two cars, my mother often accompanied my father to his office. From there, she walked to the local fish and meat markets in order to select the freshest ingredients. We even had home delivery. An Arab with a donkey brought fresh vegetables and fruits to the house. Another merchant came with staples.

Most of our meals were French-influenced, but occasionally for Sunday lunch, Mother made couscous, the North African meal served daily in Arab homes. Instead of roasting the traditional lamb or mutton, Mother used chicken as the main ingredient. She also made a beef pot roast and prepared meatballs in a tomato sauce as side dishes. Harissa, the hot sauce sprinkled over the mixture, added piquancy to the flavors. Today when I eat couscous I pile my plate high with the steamed couscous grain, perfumed with the aromas and tastes from the flavored chicken stock. Next, I add the vegetables, meats and one hardboiled egg: my mother placed eggs, still in the shell, into the bouillon. She cooked them for about 10 minutes, then peeled the shell and placed the eggs around the edges of the platter of couscous. The *torchi,* a salad of grated raw carrots and turnips, seasoned with vinegar, salt, and a bit of dried red pepper is served separately. I blend everything and with my first taste, I am transported back to my childhood in Algeria.

Let me mention the special flavor of *dipcha.* In English, this is cilantro. Once, when my mother prepared couscous for us in Paris, she returned from shopping with a small packet of *persil chinois,* or Chinese parsley, aka cilantro. She had spent a significant amount of money for this handful of greenery purchased from a specialty market. What would she think of finding an abundant supply of cilantro in San Antonio supermarkets today?

Our house sat on a large plot of land that had a tennis court, fruit trees, and a garden. Although not a traditional climate, we had fresh artichokes in Constantine. Maybe our gardener, Tahar, was particularly gifted. I can't explain it; I just remember picking fresh artichokes was one of the joys of my childhood.

I was 13 years old and my brothers, 10 and 12 when our mother developed tuberculosis. The prescribed treatment was a prolonged rest in the mountain air. This was a difficult time for everyone as my father had to work and could not care for three young active boys so I was sent to live with a cousin and my brothers were placed with a different family.

Aurette left for France after we were settled in our new homes. The trip was arduous. My father drove her to Algiers and from there she sailed on a ferry for the overnight trip to Marseille, France. Then she boarded a train for the Jura, a mountainous region near the Swiss border, to begin collapso-therapy treatment. The doctors inserted tubes into the affected lung and attached them to a pump that forced its partial collapse. Once deflated, the lung could not work, giving the organ time to heal. It was tough treatment! She spent one year in the sanitarium, separated from her husband and sons. Fortunately, the cure worked and Aurette returned to Constantine to resume her normal life. Although the disease limited her pulmonary capacity, this was not evident in 1977, when my mother, age 72, came to visit us in Colorado Springs. Every morning, she marched without difficulty up and down the hills in our neighborhood, an altitude of 6,000 feet.

Although we were Jewish, we were not particularly observant in our daily lives. My father, who was agnostic, was proud of his Jewish heritage. Few traditions were followed, but Aurette observed the Yom Kippur fast every year and Mario and I made our Bar Mitzvahs. I must confess I did not do it for noble reasons as I was promised a bicycle. I am also embarrassed to admit the rabbi had to stand behind me, coaching me during the reading of the Hebrew passages. Not a proud memory. Mario had an unhappy experience associated with the event. After the ceremony he took my bike out for a spin. However, he fell and was knocked unconscious. Fortunately, he recovered after a brief period.

As a child, the navy was my first love. I used to spend many hours drawing pictures of warships and sailing ships. My dream was to attend the French Naval Academy. (Although that did not happen, I still subscribe to and read the *Naval Proceedings* and *Naval History* each month.)

It was only after my first airplane ride that my interest in aviation began. The local Constantine airport was close, just one-half mile from our house in Sidi Mabrouk. One day, Claude's father, my Uncle David, took my cousin and me on our first flight. After that experience, I walked frequently to the airport and strolled among the planes, hoping one day to be at the controls. Eventually, the airport was moved to a larger location several miles away so my visits were confined to the weekends when our two families, who always moved in tandem, would visit the airport. From that first flight in the '30s, my interest has not waned. I am as fascinated today with aviation as I was at the age of 15, living in the middle of North Africa. Cecile, our daughter, cites an example of my fascination with planes: "Daddy was talking to another 'old retired guy' in a parking lot at Eglin Air Force Base. When they heard the sound of an aircraft engine, the other 'old retired guy' and Daddy stopped talking and both looked upwards. They watched silently until they had identified the type of plane and it had disappeared before going back to their conversation." (As an addendum to my reading choices, I have subscribed to *Aviation Week and Space Technology*, for more than 50 years.

Our lives continued with school and family routine through the late '30s until the first hints of war could no longer be ignored. We still felt safe, as we lived so far from Europe. However, in 1940, when I was 17, France fell to the German Wehrmacht. We realized our lives would change even though we didn't know the extent to which we would be affected. Still, we were fortunate, compared to those in Europe.

THREE

....

WWII
PERSPECTIVE FROM
NORTH AFRICA

For many readers, World War II is a period in history that has little current relevance. It took place too long ago and there have been too many conflicts in more recent memory that crowd out any sense of what the world went through between 1939 and 1945.

In preparing research for this book, I went back to the history books to refresh my memory, but I've always kept certain dates in my mind because these periods affected me personally.

In 1934, the Germans signed a non-aggression pact with Poland, but five years later they marched into Polish territory, effectively launching the first incursions of WWII. Nine months after that, in May 1940, the Germans invaded Holland and then began their march across the Low Countries on the way to France.

The French believed the Maginot Line, a series of concrete battle forts, gun emplacements and outposts constructed along the north and eastern parts of France facing Germany, would protect them from an invasion. Instead, the Germans broke the neutrality of Belgium, ignored the areas with the Maginot emplacements and following the same path they had used in 1914, marched from the North into the Ardennes and from there into Paris.

Both the Belgians and the French troops fought hard, but they were outnumbered and outmaneuvered. Belgium surrendered to the German Wehrmacht on May 28, 1940 and less than one month later, on June 20, 1940, France surrendered to the Germans.

As part of the ceasefire agreement, Germany took control of Paris, the northern part of France and the entire Atlantic coast. French citizens, under the supervision of the Germans, managed government affairs in the southern part of the country. The bureaucrats were installed in Vichy, a mid-sized town in the geographical center of France. Heading this government was Marshall Pétain, a hero from World War I.

Almost immediately after the signing of the Armistice, a resistance movement sprang up both in Vichy-controlled France and the North. My cousin, Jean Pierre-Bloch, a Socialist politician, had served as a member of the French provincial government before the war. He enlisted in the French Army in 1939, but, after the fall of France, he was arrested and jailed as a member of the defeated forces. A short time later, Pierre-Bloch escaped from prison and with Gabrielle, his wife, joined the *Résistance* in Marseille. Together, the couple worked tirelessly against the Boche—an unflattering term used to describe the German occupiers. The Pierre-Blochs organized the first parachute drop of agents and fighters into the French countryside in 1941. Eventually, both were arrested on treason charges and held in a Marseille prison. Gaby, who was released after three months, began a campaign to free her husband. She smuggled saws, money, and keys in packages of food into the prison. Thanks to Gaby's efforts, Pierre-Bloch and eight British pilots who were in the same prison escaped in July 1942. Shortly after this episode, my cousin managed to fly to London where he joined General Charles de Gaulle, the leader of the Free French movement. Pierre-Bloch remained in England as head of the Free French counter-espionage activities until the Allies liberated North Africa. In 1942, he returned to Algiers where he served as Assistant Minister of the Interior for the French government in exile.

Throughout the war, Jean Pierre-Bloch and Gabrielle Bloch were instrumental in aiding the French as they struggled to regain their country. The Pierre-Blochs were patriots and heroes for France. After the war ended, the couple received multiple well-deserved awards and honors.

When scores were settled at the conclusion of the Occupation, many collaborators, particularly those who had worked for the Vichy regime, were tried and executed. Marshall Pétain escaped this fate because of his advanced age and his record of gallant war deeds in WWI. Jean Pierre-Bloch was a member of the jury that convicted the former Vichy leader. Pétain, who was imprisoned on a Brittany coastal island, remained there until his death at the age of 95 in 1951.

I had few relatives in France and none in the German-occupied northern half of the country. However, several cousins lived in Nice, on the Côte d'Azur, or as Americans know it, the Riviera. Alex Daninos, a pharmacist, like my mother, was born in Tunisia. He was married to Anna Namia and his father was my grandfather's brother. Anna and her sister Josette were the children of Cecile, my father's only sister. Because they were Jewish and living under the Vichy regime in Nice, Alex and Anna decided it would be prudent to send their two young children, Jean-Michel and Nicole, to a remote region for safekeeping. My cousin Josette, not yet married, took them to the Jura, the same region where my mother had undergone tuberculosis treatment 10 years earlier. Josette, a good Jewish girl, told us she attended Mass with the children every Sunday. She remembered the excitement on the night of the Armistice when she danced in the village streets with a member of the Maquis. (These men and women were part of a rural Résistance movement in France. The name is taken from the wild scrub plants found in Corsica and the South of France.) Many of the Macquis were Communists, but they were also outstanding spies and saboteurs, and they played a vital role in fighting the occupiers.

Since we were living in North Africa, I think we always believed the events in Europe would not affect us. At home in Constantine, the official propaganda station was Radio Vichy, but when the broadcast was not blocked by the government, our parents, who were ardent Gaullistes, listened to the BBC and followed General Charles de Gaulle's attempts to organize the Forces Françaises Libre, the Free French Forces. Although, the British acknowledged De Gaulle as the leader of the French government in exile, President Franklin Roosevelt preferred to ignore this edict. FDR was successful in his efforts to keep De Gaulle from going into North Africa for the campaign that signaled the start of the Allied return to Europe.

I was still living at home after the Vichy regime took over the government. There were changes in our lives, but in reality my family was fortunate. The Vichy government did not have the resources to completely isolate the Jewish population, so although rules were instigated regarding Jews, they were not as restrictive or as strictly enforced at the level found in German-occupied France or even in the southern Vichy portion of the country.

In Algeria a quota policy was implemented. The French, being less informal than the Americans, called the rule by its Latin meaning, Numerus Clausus or Number Limited. In our *lycée* or high school, Jewish children were removed and placed in separate schools run by Jewish teachers. I suspect the elders in the Consistoire, the governing body for Jewish citizens, organized these new schools. In the Algerian schools, these tactics should have affected me; however, my brothers, our cousins and I were exempt from this Vichy ruling. We were allowed to remain in our lycée and continue our studies since Georges and his brother David had been decorated for bravery during WWI.

Although, there are probably no survivors left today from the 1914-1918 period, in the mid 20th century, this conflict still had special meaning for the French. Veterans were treated with great respect and honor. Our own Veteran's Day, observed on November 11, the same day as the other WWI allies, has never been held over to a make a three-day weekend. This remembrance of the Armistice, signed on the 11th hour of the 11th day of the 11th month acknowledges the terrible sacrifices of the soldiers who served in the 1914-1918 conflict.

In 1942, I was completing the first *stage* or part of my Baccalauréate. French students must pass two separate exams before they can attend a university. Generally, each part takes one year to complete. My studies for the Bac were the Première Partie, a general exam that covered French literature, mathematics, geography, and language, in my case, English. I passed the test successfully!

Our lives changed with the launch of Operation Torch, the Allied invasion to retake the Axis-controlled regions of North Africa. The fighting, which began November 8, 1942, and ended two days later, drove the Axis troops from the cities of Casablanca, Algiers, and Oran. From these victories, the Allies marched east to meet the British forces in Tunisia, Libya, and Egypt. Several months later they defeated Rommel's Afrika Korps forces and forced the Axis troops to retreat into Sicily. Approximately one year earlier, the Germans had successfully pushed the Allies from Tunisia and Libya in the first North Africa encounter so winning this territory back was particularly important.

After the liberation of Algiers and Oran, the Allies passed through Constantine on the way to Tunisia and Egypt. I was excited! I wanted to practice my English skills so as the Americans approached the city I rode my bicycle to the outskirts of town. It was a big day for all of us. I waved and spoke with the soldiers as they passed in their lightly armed trucks emblazoned with the large white star on the sides. They set up an operations center not far from our house in Sidi Mabrouk. Over the next few weeks we met several American soldiers and British officers. My brother and I were allowed to invite them for lunch and dinner. They came, bringing food and cigarettes as gifts. At the time, my mother, who smoked occasionally, preferred the blond cigarettes the British brought. They were preferable to the dark Gauloises or other tobacco available in this area.

Although my brother Mario and I spoke some English and served as the family interpreters, my skills had limits. I remember trying to figure out the difference between the soldier who came from I-OWA and the one who was from O-HI-O.

In May 1943, even though the North African campaign had ended, the Vichy regime still controlled our lives. I was drafted and assigned to a special Jewish unit, but I didn't realize my role in the war was different until I arrived at the induction center in Constantine's large caserne or army base. When I looked around and noticed my fellow conscripts, even the sergeant, was Jewish; I realized our participation in the war effort would be limited.

This caserne had always been a part of the city. As a child, I watched the soldiers ride their horses during exercises and parades. Now, I was to be part of it, just not on horseback. As Jews, we were not allowed to carry arms, so we could not be in the infantry or artillery. Our roles and duties were supportive, non-combat only. Most of us drove trucks or staff cars and delivered supplies.

As a trainee, I was assigned to a transport unit at the caserne. There I learned to drive in a convoy; maybe because I loved all motorized vehicles, I didn't mind the assignment.

I was a Zouave conscript. Zouave units, created for Algerian forces in the early 1800s, had an impressive campaign history. The soldiers, known as fearless fighters, wore distinctive colorful uniforms, easily recognizable in any photo or painting. Vincent Van Gogh, the Dutch artist, painted several portraits of Zouave soldiers dressed in the traditional balloon pants, fez, and leggings. By the time my brother Yvan donned the uniform, the colorful costume had become more subdued. Yvan had a *chechiya*, which you can see on his photo, and although he is carrying a rifle, and wearing leggings with a strap, it's some distance from the famous colors and original design used earlier.

Guy Castel, a friend of Yvan who joined our family after he married my cousin Maude, has this on-the-ground recollection of the WWII Zouave uniform:

> It's very difficult to find color photos of them because, after their creation in Algeria in the 19th century, they were disbanded following the Second World War. Anyway,

they were imitated in many countries, including during the U.S. Civil War because of their reputation of bravery and dash. Regretfully, in the process, many details of their uniform were modified, keeping only their characteristic fez, open-fronted jacket, long sash and baggy trousers.

I was drafted in the Air Force by General de Gaulle's temporary government in Algiers two years after Gino. The French barracks were extremely poor in material. So I was given heavy shoes, a blue overcoat which had been used in the 1914-1918 war and a rifle Lebel 1907-model for drill. Of course, for socks, I received the famous 'putties,' that long band of cloth that took at least 20 minutes to put on, a time sufficient for a Wehrmacht company to occupy a whole city.

As always, we believed General de Gaulle would arrive and we could fight with him. Any indignity we suffered was always with this thought and belief.

FOUR

....

I WAS A DESERTER

War doesn't go in a straight line. Battles are won and lost. Territory is gained and later given up. Weather affects outcomes. The political realities pursued by government leaders, including generals and admirals, cannot be ignored in winning or losing a war.

President Franklin Roosevelt disliked Charles de Gaulle's overwhelming personality. De Gaulle believed he alone carried the responsibility for the survival of France. He was the only French leader who organized a fighting force outside occupied French territory and he was prepared to assist and lead in taking back his country from the Germans. Churchill, who was more disposed to accept De Gaulle's role, still found him difficult, and in a famous quote said, "The greatest cross I have to bear is the Croix de Lorraine." Lorraine refers to the province where General de Gaulle made his home.

In the last chapter, I mentioned the British and American soldiers who passed through Constantine as part of Operation Torch.

As further explanation, in 1942, after three years of war in Europe, the Allies began their return to the European mainland with Operation Torch. De Gaulle's single-mindedness and difficult personality led President Roosevelt and General Dwight Eisenhower, as the U.S. forces commander, to keep De Gaulle from assuming a leadership role in this operation. Instead, the Allies chose Admiral François Darlan, the Vichy French leader in North Africa. In the eyes of most of the French, Darlan was a traitor to his country, but the Allies believed he was the only French leader who could keep the Vichy French troops stationed in Algeria, Morocco, and Tunisia from fighting against the invading forces.

There was discord and enmity on all sides dating back two years before the start of Operation Torch. After the fall of France, the British had warned the French Navy to move their ships docked at the Mers-el-Kebir harbor in Oran, Algeria, to a distant French naval base in Dakar. The Allies, led by the British, did not want the Germans to commandeer these ships, fearing they could be used against American and British forces, either for transport of men and supplies or as fighting ships. The French ignored the warning. Three days after the edict, the British bombed the ships in the harbor, destroying most of the fleet and killing 1,400 French sailors. The French resented, and indeed hated, the British for their attack on Mers-el-Kebir.

As preparations for Operation Torch began, the Allies realized the British could not persuade the Vichy French forces to change allegiances, so Eisenhower sent Robert Murphy, the U.S. Minister to North Africa, to negotiate with Darlan. The strategy worked, and after a few skirmishes in Algiers, the Vichy French forces withdrew from the battle. That allowed the Allies to march successfully through North Africa.

Darlan's reign was short-lived. A member of the Free French forces shot and killed him on Christmas Eve, 1942.

General Henri Giraud assumed control as the High Commissioner of French North Africa, but the Allies allowed the Vichy government to remain the law of the land. The anti-Semitic measures that had been introduced after the fall of France included the abrogation of the Décret Crémieux, the right of full citizenship for Jewish citizens remained. The reason given was that it was unfair to Muslims since they were not accorded the same privileges. It was only later after Jean Pierre-Bloch became a French official in North Africa that he was able to reinstate the Décret Crémieux.

These momentous events, including the Allied retaking of North Africa, had little effect on my military situation.

Following basic training, I was assigned to an Army base in Algiers At first, I worked around the docks, unloading heavy equipment; after that, I drove a personnel carrier, certainly more interesting work than moving boxes. Eventually, since I spoke English and because I had been trained for transport duties, I was assigned to chauffeur American officers using a prewar Chevrolet. My free time was spent with relatives who lived in Algiers. Life was quite pleasant.

On May 13, 1943, the Allies announced they had defeated the German and Italian forces in North Africa. This gave General de Gaulle an opportunity to set up his headquarters in Algiers, now a French-controlled region. The shadow government under his command remained active until the Allied landing in Normandy, June 6, 1944. Two months later, after considerable political maneuvering, General de Gaulle led the march into Paris, signaling the end of the occupation for the city.

But that was two years later. In early 1943, I was still a member of the Vichy French Army. For me, the war was far from over! France was still under German occupation. Following their defeat in North Africa, the Germans moved troops from Algeria, Morocco, and Tunisia into the southern part of France to defend what they knew would be a push by the Allies into Europe.

Not long after Operation Torch had ended, word spread through our barracks in Algiers that General de Gaulle was looking for volunteers to join the Forces. It was time to join the General! According to the instructions that we passed along, my fellow deserters and I were to wait outside the caserne for a truck. From there we would be driven to a Free French Forces mobilization center.

The word "desert" didn't have much meaning for me. Could we have been shot if we had been caught? I don't know; we had the narrow vision of youth. Our conviction was so profound that De Gaulle was the only legitimate commander to follow that no second thought was given. I'm sure I assumed I was immortal.

Late at night I left the barracks and, as instructed, waited on the street. Mario, who was a university student in Algiers, came with me, probably for brotherly support and to be able to give our parents some reassurance. Several other young men were also waiting. Eventually, an old army truck appeared, fitted with a very high freeboard and covered with a canvas tarpaulin stopped. I said goodbye to Mario and climbed aboard. As we left, we tossed away our old uniforms and donned British fatigues. Before settling down for a long night's ride, I said au revoir without regret to the Vichy French forces!

We could hear German planes bombing the harbor as we drove through the city. Although the campaign in North Africa was almost over, the Germans still attempted to interdict the unloading of supplies from the Allied ships tied at the docks.

By climbing aboard the truck, we were transformed from young deserters to recruits. We were told to sit and not show our faces. The ride was bumpy, but in the Algerian springtime the temperature was bearable. There were some provisions on board and the overall tone was one of excitement. Once we were on the road we lifted the side of the tarpaulin and watched the changing landscape. The 500-mile trip from Algiers to Kairouan, Tunisia, our induction center, took two full days and nights. Upon our arrival, we signed papers acknowledging we were volunteers for the Forces Françaises Libre (FFL). I still have the document I signed on May 23, 1943! On that day, I became a full-fledged member of De Gaulle's Free French.

When they asked me as a volunteer to choose my arms, I said, "I want to fly." That presented somewhat of a problem since the Free French forces had only a handful of planes. Most FFL flying was done as part of the British air effort.

When I grow up I want to be . . .

Now that I think about it, I find it remarkable I was taken seriously just because I said I wanted to be a pilot. Generally, armed forces are more interested in filling spaces than indulging the whims of 20-year-old boys. I was not the only one; there were 15 other young recruits, who, like me, thought a flying career would be a great way to serve our country.

It was still wartime, even though the North African campaign was almost finished. As with armies everywhere, it was hurry up and wait. Since there was only one active flying outfit for the Free French forces, and that was fully staffed, we had to wait before we could take the next step of being assigned to flight training. For the next several months, we moved from one transit camp to another. After a few weeks, we left Kairouan by truck and started our journey across Tunisia, through Libya, and then into Egypt.

Tripoli, the capital of Libya, was a beautiful city on the Mediterranean Sea. Our open truck rumbled across the desert, leaving us exposed to the hot sun and the dust, but the excitement of the trip compensated for some of the hardship. In Tripoli we were quartered in tents, not far from the sea. There were some advantages to this rustic life. Our only task was to keep our area clean and attend daily assemblies. The rest of the time we moved around freely.

A British Army Cooking School was based at our camp. As a result, meals were copious, varied, and quite acceptable; not the sort of food normally found in wartime or desert situations. On the minus side, there was an anti-aircraft battery near our camp. At night, if there were any German aircraft in the vicinity, even at a distance, sleep was impossible because of the booming guns.

We were dressed like English soldiers in summer uniforms. However, our uniforms had the patch on the left shoulder with the French tricolor. In France, we refer to our mutual colors as *bleu, blanc, rouge,* or blue, white and red, rather than the American red, white, blue. I still have my cloth patch and my pilot's wings from three Air Forces: France, United States, and Israel, each resting safely under the protection of a glass frame.

The Free French needed an air force, but for the moment, equipment was limited to whatever could be borrowed from the British. These planes were flown by a handful of French pilots who had escaped from the continent into North Africa. We were to be the next generation.

The leisurely pace to find a home for us gave rise to many rumors: were we to train in Russia for flight school? At other times, England, Canada and the U.S. were mentioned as possible destinations. We knew we would eventually be sent to Rayak Air Base at the Syri-

an-Lebanese border as an intermediate stop, but until
then and what would follow remained a mystery.

One evening while in Tripoli, I attended a Shabbat
service at the local synagogue. This visit began a lifelong habit for Charlotte and me as we have visited Sephardic synagogues in many cities. Not only do these
visits give us pleasure, they serve as a reminder of my
roots. They appear in the most unlikely spots and their
survival in many instances is nothing short of miraculous. While visiting Marrakech, Morocco, we came upon
an ancient Jewish cemetery as we prepared to enter the
medina, the old Arab quarter. Its gravestones rested at
odd angles in a nondescript sand-blown plot. Our guide
spotted a rabbi who looked almost as ancient as the
stones. Here we were in an Arab country, meeting a rabbi who happened to have startlingly clear blue eyes! He
had white hair and a bent figure. In spite of the infirmi-
ties of age, the rabbi was pleased to show us the synagogue as he related the story of its existence. It was
simple and certainly an old structure. As in so many of
these houses of worship, the Jewish population was de-
creasing with each generation.

In another synagogue on the Isle of Rhodes in the
Aegean Sea, just five families remain in a congregation
that has existed since the 16th century. All these are Sephardic synagogues. I haven't run into any other Nar-

bonis on these scouting visits, but I see names that ring a bell, most likely a branch of a family we knew from Constantine.

From Tripoli, our mode of transport changed. We boarded a ship in the harbor for the short overnight journey to Alexandria, a trip remarkable for the number of shipwrecks strewn about the harbor. The city was much neater, having been spared much of the bombardment. From Alexandria, it was a short journey to our next transit camp at the base of the Pyramids.

The atmosphere in nearby Cairo was pleasant. I found myself in familiar surroundings, not so much geographically, but socially, since I had lived all my life among Muslim crowds. Cairo was bustling, dusty, and hot; its streets filled with heavy traffic. The country was no longer under any military threat since the Italian-German coalition had been defeated and Allied troops had cleared North Africa of the Axis army.

As usual, there was a family connection in the area. This time it was the Shemylas, who owned a department store in the city. I was invited for lunch on several occasions, both in their home and in restaurants. It gave me a wonderful way to see Cairo as I was guided by local residents.

Staging areas and departure points are often positioned around temporary bases. During my time here, at the foot of the Pyramids, I shared a large tent with five other men who were also waiting to be transported to the next stage in our military life. My tent mates, like me, had expressed an interest in becoming a pilot. However, as recruits, lacking any planes or plans, we were not very high on anyone's list to secure transport to our next point, Rayak Air Base.

FIVE

....

LIFE IN LEBANON

Amazingly, in the thick of war in 1943, we had no commitments and no serious military obligations. Those from our group who had chosen the infantry or artillery fighting elements were probably already battling it out with the Germans in Italy and undoubtedly some had been wounded or killed. For us, this hiatus in the war was the result of the political machinations that eventually led to the reestablishment of General De Gaulle's leadership in North Africa, France, and its colonial holdings. Since my intent was never to skirt my duties as a French soldier, I am grateful I avoided harm during that period.

I'm not sure these were questions we pondered as we sat around the transit camp. We were eager to move to the next phase in our aviation careers. Two weeks after our arrival in Egypt, we got our wish and boarded a train for Beirut, Lebanon. Our travels took us through the vast empty expanses of the Sinai Desert. When we reached

Palestine, a part of which would become Israel a few years later, we started to see green fields and orchards. From there, our route took us across Jordan. Finally, we arrived in Beirut, the capital of Lebanon. At that point, we boarded a bus that took us to our new home at Rayak Air Base. The base was situated in the Bekaa Valley, a large fertile plain outlined by two mountain ranges running parallel to the Mediterranean Sea. The Lebanese mountains and the Anti-Lebanese mountains traverse the country from north to south.

Some historical background about the region can give a better picture of the political and geographical situation in the early part of the 20th century. At the conclusion of World War I, following the breakup of the Ottoman Empire, Lebanon and Syria became one country, which was placed under French control as a mandate and ruled by a French High Commissioner. Beirut, a beautiful and vibrant city, became known as the Paris of the East. Among the elites, a French way of life prevailed. A modernization program brought welcome changes. Roads were improved, more schools were built and a government structure and bureaucracy, *á la française*, was implemented.

The political situation was more complicated. Lebanon had both Shia and Sunni Muslims but the strong Christian Maronite minority held the favored position and made up a majority of the government. Shia and Sunni Muslims divided the remaining political power.

As with other countries in the Middle East throughout the ages, the political and geographical lines of the area have been redrawn many times. Lebanon and Syria were the first countries in the region to return to British and French control during WWII. In mid-1941, after two months of fighting in operations little known outside the area, the British Army and Air Forces, with the help of Australian troops, defeated the Axis armies. An armistice ended the Vichy regime in Lebanon and Syria.

Later that year, General de Gaulle visited Lebanon in order to strengthen his claim as the leader of French interests outside the country. While in Lebanon, he was pressed by Muslim/Lebanese leaders to end the Mandate. Although the process began slowly, most countries, including the United States, Britain, the Arab States, and the Soviet Union recognized Lebanon's claims of independence at the time of De Gaulle's visit.

What did this have to do with me? Well, not much. I just happened to be stationed in Rayak during this period. The air base had lost strategic significance, bereft of airplanes and empty, except for a small contingent of local troops, used as guards. On the opposite side of the compound, the Royal Air Force had a squadron that provided the flying support operations.

The residential buildings were serviceable and since they were recently built, quite comfortable. Our dorm building had a gently rusting anti-aircraft machine gun on the roof, a vestige from the time when the base was active and had to show some semblance of military attitude.

The British provided basic food service. Fortunately, produce and regional products supplied by local merchants gave our traditional Anglo-Saxon mess hall diet a distinct Middle Eastern flavor.

Daily duties consisted of an assembly and guard duties for the empty hangers. Rayak was a large base; the hangers were in an isolated section, about one mile from our barracks. During the overnight watch, the hangers were forbidding. The wind whistled through the girders of the hangers and we could hear the distant howls of the wolves and jackals as we rounded the buildings on our guarding detail.

Apart from these guard duties, we had few responsibilities, so we jogged and played soccer with the British troops. The schedule allowed ample time for sightseeing. We made several trips to Beirut to take advantage of the good restaurants and stroll along the shoreline that reminded us of Nice and Cannes. Walking east from the gate put us on the road to Damascus. In small towns along this route, we visited the souks, the traditional Arab covered markets, where small children no older than

10 or 12 peddled gold bracelets and earrings on trays as if they were candy or peanuts.

Zahle was a particularly attractive village nestled in the mountains between Rayak and Beirut. A stream, its banks lined with cafes, provided a lovely place to rest. Coffee, sweet drinks, and finger foods were served under the shade of orange trees and date palms.

After spending what I am sure were several weeks of boring guard duty, we decided to stretch our hitchhiking thumbs and venture farther from the base. I joined about 10 of my fellow recruits on a visit to Baalbek, the site of ancient ruins in the Bekaa Valley. One morning, we just walked off the base and hitchhiked to the site about 15 miles away. As this was wartime, anyone wearing a uniform could find a ride without difficulty. We spent the day seeing the sights of Baalbek never thinking we might have a problem returning to the base. However, at night, there was little traffic on the road so we had to walk the entire distance. We didn't have papers nor had we gotten permission to leave, which meant we could not return through the main gate. Instead, we climbed a fence and returned to our barracks, unscathed and unseen. We were lucky. No one had reported us missing and the next day we resumed our normal, boring duties.

I did not have much interest in the political realities involved with a new government being formed under my nose. Not wanting to wait any longer, in November 1943, the new Lebanese cabinet members took matters into their own hands and amended the Constitution, abolishing the articles that referred to the Mandate. The French responded by arresting prominent politicians, hoping they could retain control of the country.

The situation became tense.

Enter Narboni, the "peacekeeper." We, the raw recruits and aviators-in-waiting, were issued rifles and sent from Rayak to patrol the streets of Beirut. Apparently, we were successful in keeping the peace because after a few days we returned to the base and resumed our humdrum existence of waiting for an assignment.

Meanwhile, in Constantine, my mother was writing letters, trying to help her son secure an assignment to flight school. Mothers everywhere, and they don't have to be Jewish, are usually willing to do just about anything to help their children.

It was mid-1943. As I mentioned in the preceding chapter, our cousin Jean Pierre-Bloch, following his escape from prison worked directly for Charles de Gaulle in London. After the Allies liberated North Africa, Pierre-Bloch became the Assistant Minister of the Interior in Algiers. At last we had a relative with influence!

Mother, in her quest for my advancement, had written to Pierre-Bloch without my knowledge. I have no confirmation or proof that he was responsible for my assignment, but given the circumstances of the following story, I have to say it's a likely scenario.

At the camp, boredom had set in. Don't ask me why, but I decided to go to Palestine. Was it my Jewish heritage that made me want to see Jerusalem and the ancient lands? Was it because I had never been to this part of the world? For whatever reason, I just had to go. I guess I shouldn't wonder why, when my daughters were younger and wanted to do certain things, they never worried about the outcomes of their actions. It's in the genes.

Perhaps this is the time to mention that, again, I went without proper paperwork, in other words, AWOL, or absent without leave. It's like deserting the Vichy French Army. I must not have thought about the consequences. When you're young, you can do anything!

I took off to visit the land of my ancestors, staying on the road for about one week. Upon reflection, I probably thought I wouldn't be missed. I hitchhiked, even though I had money for food and lodging. I visited Tel Aviv, Jerusalem, Bethlehem, the Red Sea, Haifa, and points in between, spending several nights at the U.S.O. in Tel Aviv. Charlotte always asks if girls were involved. Really, that's one of the blessings of age; I don't know, but, if pushed for a response, I would probably say, yes, I met girls along the way.

Speaking of girls, I remember another component of life at Rayak. There was an official *brothel militaire* next to the base. It was sanctioned and controlled and the girls were subject to health reviews. The soldiers were also required to undergo physical exams and testing. This is one base activity in which I did not participate!

To continue my Palestine travel story, I returned to base, and having the cockiness of any young man, went through the gate believing nothing would happen to me. Unfortunately, I had been missed, and no, they would not overlook my weeklong absence. I was unceremoniously thrown in jail.

It was not pleasant. The jail consisted of one large unheated room for all the miscreants. Toilet and bathing facilities were minimal. There were no bunks. We slept on the concrete floor with nothing but a blanket for cover. As it was mid-November, the mountain weather was chilly. After spending several days locked up, someone came into the jail and yelled, "Narboni, gather up your belongings! You're leaving!"

This is where my mother reenters the story. I think I realized these words were a good omen as I had received a letter from her before my incarceration, telling me she had contacted Pierre-Bloch. Apparently, a mother's wish carries weight because a U.S.-made plane, a Lockheed Hudson, had arrived to pick me up!

Can you imagine? Here I was, 20 years old, in jail, and an airplane filled with French officials swings by a remote base in Lebanon to fetch me. There wasn't much time; I packed my gear and climbed aboard. The bumpy ride had the distinction of being the only time in my life I was airsick. We landed in Libya and spent the night in a transit camp before flying to Casablanca the following morning. There, I took the first steps to become an aviator.

Our destination was Cazes, an airfield in Casablanca, Morocco, used by both the French and the Americans. This was my second initiation into military life, but I did not care since I had a clear destination. I was on my way to pilot training in the United States! We were to be part of a special group of airman training with American pilots, and eventually earning U.S. pilot wings. This was exciting news.

First there was aptitude, physical and psychological testing. We spent two weeks filling out forms, learning to drill, and getting used to military life. For the next several months, I lived and worked in a unit with about 75 Frenchmen. Most, like me, including several other Jewish boys, came from North Africa, but a few recruits had escaped from France and had made their way to Algeria or Morocco.

Finally, the time for departure arrived. We were sent to Oran, Algeria, where we boarded the *U.S.S. Mariposa,* an ocean liner that had been converted to a troop ship. Since German U-boats were prowling the North Atlantic looking for Allied shipping and troop vessels to sink, many slow Allied ships traveled in a convoy with armed ships acting as escorts.

But, the *Mariposa*, a passenger steamship, was a faster vessel so we could zigzag across the North Atlantic without any naval support.

Other Allied troops were also on board the *Mariposa*. As it was wartime and we were recruits, conditions were not luxurious. In our cabin we had eight berths, four on each side, one above another. We had some duties, but again, trying to fill the days took most of our time. The work schedule was light and mostly forgettable.

My one unforgettable memory comes from a stupid act. The ship's store sold cigarettes to the troops. In those days, they were readily available and very cheap. I didn't smoke, nor had I ever smoked. Because of my father's war wounds and his weakened pulmonary state, tobacco was not permitted in our house so I had never been tempted. However, out of boredom, or maybe because I thought it was the thing to do, I bought a pack. One night while on deck, I pulled out a cigarette and lit it with a match. Everyone within range jumped on me and doused my cigarette. How stupid I was; we were, of course, in total darkness. The blackout was rigorously enforced and here I was about to create a light for any nearby submarine to spot. I learned my lesson.

SIX

....

FLIGHT SCHOOL IN AMERICA

Landing in Boston Harbor in September 1944 remains an important milestone in my life. Although I did not realize it at the time, this is where I began to live the American Dream. I don't know why, but I knew the United States was different and very special.

First things first: World War II was not over, although, by late 1944 the tide had turned in the Allies' favor. Paris had been liberated and France was again free. General de Gaulle, who had returned to Paris, was recognized as the Provisional President of France. The Allies prepared to move into Germany and meet up with the Russian forces arriving from the East, but a long, difficult winter remained before victory would be assured. The Battle of the Bulge, Hitler's last desperate attempt to break up the British and U.S. forces marching toward Germany, began in the Ardennes in mid-December and lasted through January 1945. It was the largest battle of the war, resulting in many wounded

57

soldiers and deaths on both sides. Even with this German defeat, the war in Europe did not end until May 1945.

The battles in the Pacific were still raging in the fall of 1944. During this period, the Allies fought difficult and bloody campaigns as they crossed the Pacific. In addition to smaller islands, the Allies recaptured Okinawa and the Philippines in preparation for the expected invasion of Japan.

Those of us just beginning our training as pilots could not see an end to the war. We truly believed we would be part of it.

As recruits, we were given the enlisted rank of sergeant upon our arrival in the United States. It took more than one year to rotate through the programs at five air bases and schools before we became pilots and received an officer's rank. Today, I look back and marvel. How did we, so young and so naïve, learn to fly a plane?

Rereading a letter I wrote to my parents in 1945 when I was 22 years old reminds me our transformation from sergeant-recruits of the Free French forces to twin-engine bomber pilots or single-engine fighter pilots was nothing short of miraculous. That achievement, along with the determination and skill of the officers and enlisted men of the United States Army Air Corps who trained us, made a dream come true.

When I grow up I want to be . . .

PRE-FLIGHT SCHOOL FOR PILOTS

Craig Field, Selma, Alabama. Our American journey began with a two-day, two-night train trip from Boston to Selma, Alabama. We had a low priority among the other troops and equipment moving by train so we stopped frequently along the way, sitting and waiting in our train cars for permission to move onto a different track that would take us closer to our destination. Finally, we arrived.

Our training began at the Pre-Flight School for Pilots, Craig Field, Selma, Alabama. The recruits slated to be mechanics, engineers, and radio operators went to schools at different bases. Those of us in the pilot group began a difficult six-week period of study. First, there were English lessons. Although we loved Hollywood films, we were a group of 21-year-olds, living in an era without the daily immersion of American TV and videos. Imagine our challenge to become proficient, quickly, in a foreign language. Understanding and speaking English was essential to our survival and to the instructor pilots who flew with us! My English was acceptable, thanks to an excellent high school teacher. As I had worked for British and American soldiers I was comfortable with the language. The same could not be said for most of my fellow recruits. I don't know how they managed since in those days, few Americans could speak a second language. From what I've read about our training program, the staff searched for any instructor pilot who could speak French. I think they used Cajuns in some instances. This may sound snobbish, but for those of us born in France, the Canadian or Cajun version of French does not meet our standards. In some cases, it's unrecognizable to us.

Our classes included English language training, PT or physical training, basic flying mechanics, and identifying friendly and enemy aircraft. We were issued new uniforms, received our first pay and drank our first bottle of Coca-Cola. It was, after all, the South.

The training was intensive. Anyone who did not measure up, either because of physical handicaps, inadequate eyesight being the most common, or who could not learn the basics of navigation, radio operation or other requirements would not be allowed to continue the path toward earning the coveted pilot's wings. These recruits would be transferred to navigator or mechanical training programs. I don't think that philosophy has changed much in the intervening years. The physical and mental standards to become a pilot remain stringent.

Our social life was limited. As far as girls were concerned, we were taken by bus into Birmingham and introduced to members of the French Club. Don't ask me anymore than that. I don't remember.

When I grow up I want to be . . .

PRIMARY TRAINING

Hawthorne School of Aeronautics, Orangeburg, South Carolina. We survived our first school and moved on to our 10-week Primary Training course at Hawthorne School of Aeronautics, Orangeburg, South Carolina. Here's where we got into real flying! Every morning we flew with our instructor, who sat in the back with a second set of controls. We used the PT-17, a two-seater Primary Trainer built by Boeing, for our excursions into the wild blue yonder.

This plane, produced in large numbers during WWII, had a second life as a crop duster after the war. A search of the Internet brings up Web addresses that still sell model plane kits and radio-controlled versions of the PT-17. It was a very forgiving airplane, which was the most important reason for its popularity. You could get away with doing stupid things, the type of equipment the U.S. Army Air Corps needed in which to train 21-year-olds. There was one caveat for the PT-17: if you weren't paying attention during landing you could have a problem. The plane, which is supposed to taxi in a straight line during rollout can make a ground loop or turn around in a circle. This wasn't particularly dangerous but it was embarrassing. Fortunately, this never happened to me.

In the afternoon, our ground school classes included map reading, navigation, mechanics of flight, more English lessons, Morse code for the radio, and of course, PT. At night we reviewed the day's material and prepared for the exams at the end of the 10-week period.

As students who had not yet made the all-important solo flight, we could be easily identified: we wore our flight goggles reversed or perched on the back of our heads. After we soloed, when we weren't using them in the cockpit, we kept them facing forward.

That special day arrived for me November 14, 1944 . . . *solo flight!*

One day while I was sitting in the front seat the instructor said, "Narboni, you'll solo tomorrow." I think any pilot remembers this experience.

First, let me say, my solo flight went well. Tradition rules the day for this milestone. Upon landing, we were met by our classmates and doused with a bucket of water. But, for me, the real memory for this special occasion came with preparing my short-snorter. My instructor signed his name on a dollar bill, then the vital data from the flight was added; the plane's number, make, model, and the date of the flight was inscribed along on the border of the dollar. Instructions for maintaining the integrity of this procedure was always the same: I am required to carry this bill in case I meet the instructor. If he asks to see it and I can't produce it, I will have to buy him a drink or shot, known as a short-snorter. I am pleased to say that if I should happen to run into my instructor, I am prepared. My short-snorter is in my wallet as it has been for 69 years!

BASIC TRAINING

Gunter Field Montgomery, Alabama. At the end of 10 weeks, we moved to Montgomery, Alabama, for Basic Training at Gunter Field, the third stop on our flight school journey. By the time I went through the program, significant progress in aviation technology had been made. Our class used the newly arrived AT-6 trainer. This plane, substantially more complicated, had variable propeller pitch, retractable landing gear and standard radio communications. All these new capabilities allowed us to learn more advanced skills in less time. Again, we had to solo in the new trainer. Our 10-week Gunter Field experience included training in instrument flying, aerobatics, night flying, and navigation. The routine was much the same: flying in the morning or at night and classroom work in the afternoon.

Initially, I had some difficulty with instrument flying so I was required to do a "check ride" with an instructor, which I passed. Apart from this one episode, I think I had a natural aptitude for flying and believed I had the right stuff.

Hot means hot, except when you translate directly into French. When we did something well during one of our flights, we thought we were "hot" pilots, but our instructor, an American, knew the French word for hot was *chaud* so instead, he would say, "Hey, you're a "chaud" pilot!" We thought this was terribly funny.

At Gunter we had our first experience with night flying. It was serious business because we had to fly within certain limits. None of the borders were marked; it was the sky after all. It gave a feeling of exhilaration and at the same time required close attention to not stray outside the boundaries.

I still remember my call sign. When flying, I identified myself and my aircraft with a combination of letters and numbers: Yvonne, Denise, *neuf-cinq*. Of course, I had to say it in English, Yvonne, Denise, 9-5; but born French, I still count in my mother tongue.

Before we left Gunter, we were asked to choose our arms again. This time, we had the choice of single-engine fighter planes or twin-engine bombers. I envisioned myself as an airline pilot after the war so I chose the bomber training.

By then we'd been in America for six months, the halfway mark through the program. I was a member of the Class of 45-C. Ask any U.S. Air Force pilot from this era when they graduated and he will give you a number and letter: 42-A, 43, B, and so on. As we were a single French unit, we knew only other French students, but I've often played the pilot version of the game, "What class were you in?" The number is the year and the letter is the time of the year, "A" being the first class and so on. A new class entered each segment of the program when the preceding class completed it. Those of us from Casablanca stayed together until final graduation, except for the men who did not make it. The attrition rate was high. At the completion of the course, we had about 30% fewer pilots than when we had started our journey in Boston. Those who didn't make it were assigned to other jobs: navigators, armament technicians, mechanics or radio operators. All but the navigators remained as non-commissioned officers. Those who made it to pilot designation were further divided into pilots and copilots. No question, it was all about skill that determined where one fit into the hierarchy.

ADVANCED TRAINING

Turner Field, Albany, Georgia. In Advanced Training at Turner Field we were confronted with flying a much larger, heavier airplane than we had experienced in Basic. As part of an experiment, we were to be trained in the B-25, using a complete crew. We followed the same schedule, with mornings devoted to flying, school in the afternoon, and flying again at night.

If you were to ask my favorite part of flying, I'd have to say instrument flying would be at the top, despite that one incident at Gunter Field. When you are relying on the instruments, you are closer to the airplane and the data keeps you safe and on course.

Thinking about learning to fly in 1944, and the technique needed for today's jets, I wondered which exercise was more difficult; flying WWII airplanes or today's sophisticated aircraft. I decided to ask an expert pilot, Major General Craig Gourley, USAF, for an opinion. We have known Craig since he was nine years old. He's a "chaud" pilot in the best sense of the word; I'd fly with him anywhere! When I asked him if he thought it was harder to learn to fly today than in my time, he replied without hesitation, "It was much more difficult back then. The planes today have a lot of redundancy and they are much more forgiving. The planes you flew were more difficult to operate and it took much more skill."

As we progressed in our flight training, our horizons broadened, literally. We started flying cross-country. Cross-country doesn't really mean flying across the entire country, but it's part of the lingo of any pilot. It implies a longer flight than just going up, flying around and landing. We were introduced to these cross-country flights at Turner. Again, for a young man from North Africa, the vastness of America from the air was a sight to behold. From Turner in Georgia, we would often fly north to Pittsburgh and then on to Detroit. For a trip of this length, we'd probably land once for fuel. The B-25 was a heavy, slow plane with an air speed about 225 miles per hour. In those days, that was warp speed for a young man.

I had an easy time at Turner. This was a special base and a special time for us, because here we received our pilot's wings during the May 23, 1945, graduation day parade!

OPERATIONAL AIRCRAFT TRAINING

Dodge City, Kansas. Our next stop was Dodge City, Kansas, for another 10-week training program. This was Operational Aircraft Training and for the first time we flew the B-26. It was a difficult plane to fly and was known as the widow-maker. (I think there's an airplane in every country's inventory that carries this soubriquet.) The plane had electrically operated propellers. They had a tendency to run away while you were still on the ground or even after you were airborne. When this happened, one of the propellers turned at a different rate than the other, making the airplane difficult to control. It was always a surprise when it happened. The propeller that was running away slowed down and the plane would be in danger of yawing or turning about its vertical axis.

At Dodge City, the routine was more of the same. We flew in the mornings, attended class in the afternoon, then we flew again at night. As we took more trips, we gained familiarity with American terrain.

By now, we were comfortable with the language, the life and the American spirit, so comfortable that while on a cross-country trip to Frederick, Oklahoma, we went to Dallas, Texas, for a weekend. I wish I could report some incredible experience from that jaunt, but I doubt seriously anything remarkable happened, other than we boarded the bus and returned to Frederick on time. As Frenchmen we were pretty tame.

What did I remember about our time in Kansas? Mostly that it was flat. The terrain allowed us to do some low flying, so low that we were not above "buzzing" cars on the highway. Again, high jinks à la 22-year-olds in 1945.

CREW TRAINING

Selfridge Army Air Field, Michigan. There was one more stop to make. We spent the sixth and final part of our pilot training at Selfridge Field, outside Detroit. We were there from mid-August to late December 1945.

Here we formed crews. As the pilot of "my" B-26, I had a copilot, a navigator and a radioman. Our training program included cross-country trips and simulated bombing runs. As the leader of the team, I was responsible for the group. I had to learn how to judge crewmembers' reactions to stress in the air and to conduct the mission successfully. Although not the only member of

the team, I still had the responsibility for the safety of
the crew and equipment. Again, a good learning exercise
and the first of many that I have faced, but at age 22, it
was particularly challenging, as it required total concentration. Once on the ground, we returned to our usual
camaraderie without the stress of completing a team
mission, although I was closer to the other pilots in the
group. This might have been one of those situations
where those of us who had the same challenges tended
to seek each other out in non-flying situations.

Although I was still young, like so many of the World
War II generation, I had to grow up quickly. Here I was,
flying a plane, with the responsibility for a crew as well.
In a letter to my parents that I have reread at the age of
90, I am amazed that I could have such serious thoughts:

> Only about 20 hours left; night flying and
> little of instrument flying and I shall have
> the reward. Last night I flew a "short" trip of
> 1,200 kilometers. This is what is known as a
> "cross-country." Above the sea, then harbors
> full of innumerable lights, lined up. All
> those lives flickering very far under me who
> therefore is a soul apart, [It makes more
> sense in French.] The great somber "noth-
> ing" where my airplane penetrates while
> growling

Until now, I told you very little about what I'm doing because I was not disposed to appreciate this work sufficiently to paint an agreeable picture. I have flown with my nerves and my head, not yet with my senses. I think that it (flying) is very pleasant because sometimes I have delicious reflections that come and go. Until I think again of the airplane and find myself again in my preoccupied state, we are asked to learn a maximum of things in a minimum of time to adapt in a few hours to type of airplanes which are different one from another, to become in one word, "indefatigable". Some fall ill, others are perpetually tired, but the great majority are admirable, maintaining the effort marvelously, singing, laughing, going out when it is allowed. One is then allowed to believe that they want with all their hearts that which others very quickly would have given up. There are many "washed out"—around one-third since we began.

We had a number of missions to complete at Selfridge. At the successful conclusion of these flying tasks, we were promoted to *aspirant*. This would be the equivalent of a warrant officer in the U.S. Army today. Not quite an officer, not quite enlisted.

At each base, the social life gave us opportunities to meet townspeople. While we were at Selfridge, a kind American woman took us under her wing, inviting us frequently to her home for lunch. I still have photos with our hostess. It was extremely kind of her to ask us, lonely young men, far away from home, for a home-cooked meal.

Monumental events occurred during our time at Selfridge. On April 12, 1945, President Franklin Roosevelt passed away. Just 32 days later, on May 8, 1945, the Germans surrendered to the Allies and the war in Europe was over. In August, Charles de Gaulle came to Selfridge for a brief visit. There was no formal parade; we simply gathered around General de Gaulle as he spoke to us. Can you imagine? The man for whom all of us in Algeria were counting on to save France, particularly those of us who were Jewish, was standing in front of us.

If you had asked me then about my impression of America, I would say Americans were honest and hard working and treated foreigners well. Even though I couldn't figure out how, I knew I would like to return and become an American citizen someday.

Before that happened, I had to face the reality of a return to devastated postwar France. In a letter to my parents, I expressed my concern about going back.

> Life in France, I am told, extremely difficult and expensive. Food is still scarce and

clothing cannot be found. The future is troubled from several viewpoints. Is it possible that the Jews are forgotten? Is it that people have understood, after so much suffering and communal heroism it would be an aberration and shameful loss of direction to start a fight again that will never be settled?

SEVEN

....

RETURN TO FRANCE
1946-1948

As I reflect on my life for this memoir, I realize that dividing episodes into chronological chapters makes sense. It also helps me realize how I made decisions. My life was completely unsettled as a result of the war, but I was one of the lucky ones. I not only survived, I avoided combat; and my family, still based in far away Algeria, had been spared the fate of so many others, both Jews and non-Jews.

Following our graduation from pilot training, we could say that we were pilots, but we still lacked a commercial or transport license, which I would need because I wanted to fly for the airlines. As soon as I returned to France, I signed up for the written test and passed it without difficulty.

We had been demobilized in early 1946, but I remained in the French Air Force Reserves. According to my pilot logbooks, I flew many missions from Le Bourget, the airport in Paris where Charles Lindbergh landed in 1927.

What to do next? I thought I could resume my flying career. I applied to Air France and was accepted, but first I had to report for additional commercial airline training.

And there was still the issue of my education. Before being inducted into the Vichy French Forces, I had completed the first part of a two-year process to obtain my Baccalauréate degree, the French equivalent of the first two years in an American university. Upon my return from the US, I took the philosophy section, the second part of the Baccalauréate exam. In postwar Europe, many courses like this were available in an accelerated program. I had been away from school for four years but I studied diligently and passed the Bac successfully.

All these events were happening in the same time period. In addition to taking the Bac, flying for the Reserves, and applying to the airlines, I was under pressure from my family, particularly my father, to enroll in medical school. As with all my endeavors, my parents had agreed to support me during school, so I made a decision. Instead of keeping the appointment for my Air France interview and subsequent training program, I made plans, instead, to enter the University of Paris Medical School.

That meant I still had to complete more courses before I could start the six-year path to obtain a medical degree. I had to take the PCB, the Physics/Chemistry/Biology courses and exams as part of a pre-medicine program. Again, in postwar France, the course was accelerated. It was very difficult! In letters to my parents, I lamented the work that I had to do to prepare. Surprisingly, even though I was worried, I ended up in sixth place out of eighteen.

Let me not forget to give immense credit to my parents. I had no job and only a partial education. Yet, each month, they sent me a stipend of approximately $500.

I believe I have always had good fortune throughout my life. This was certainly true when I returned to postwar Paris. I lived at the Cité Universitaire, the University of Paris campus. As with most city colleges, undergraduate or graduate housing is often inadequate. At Cité Universitaire there were about a dozen residences built and maintained by other countries to house their students studying in Paris. By French law, a number of the rooms in these *maisons* were allocated and rented to French students.

Mario lived in the Maison Belge, (Belgium House) while he attended law school. As he has helped me so many times, he arranged for me to rent a room in the same building. The Maison Belge was a particularly popular house because each student had a separate room. Meal tickets could be bought in advance and used in the student dining hall. The management even had the occasional free buffet for the students. Imagine how important this was to us if I still remember it as part of my stay.

The year was 1947. Shortages for food and fuel remained. In a request for money from my parents, I noted, "The Director requested 4,000 FF," or one month's rent, "in advance to pay for the coal." Hot water was available for one hour in the morning and one hour at night. I might add that in this case, *plus ça change, plus c'est la meme chose.*. The more things change, the more they stay the same. In 1958-1960 during my third stay at Maison Belge when I finally completed medical school, the same hot water schedule was in effect.

Letters to my parents paint a not-very-rosy picture of life in postwar Paris. Rationing was still in effect. My mother sent care packages to augment the privations of the market. Can you imagine someone in Paris needing a care package? It must have been a bad time! To give you an example of my pleas to my mother:

> As far as packages are concerned: butter and coffee, the butter less because the trip is not very good for it. Honey, yes. Jam is in free sale (not rationed) but one has to pay 150 FF for a small jar of 1/2-1 pound. I think it's too much. Continue to send milk, above all. Butter is less important. Ten cans of milk cost 100 FF. I am awaiting the bill for

cheese. It should be half from the package, although Mario, not very rich, will pay you half of it. But, for the box of milk in the future, I shall ask you to retain the amount on the monthly stipend. [In other words, I was asking her to reduce my stipend by the cost of the milk that she sent.] Yvan's ration card is exhausted! No more chocolate! But, I have a trick. Send us a few bars that I shall pay for and I shall exchange them for French chocolate bars.

This last statement deserves explanation. Apparently, the French preferred to use a certain type of chocolate in cooking, so I asked my mother to send this type and I would exchange it for the "eating bar" I preferred. Anyone who knows me understands chocolate is an extremely important part of my life as it was even when rationed. In another letter I wrote:

This morning received the jam; I think that Mario has already told you about four boxes of milk that arrived from Constantine and six boxes of milk from Tunis. How good it is to drink a good cup of coffee before leaving in the morning and another one at four o'clock

In this case I was talking about the milk, not the coffee. The coffee was another subject.

Always a meager ration. Cheese; 200 grams per person for the entire month! The chocolates—impossible to find. Powdered milk from the States. 159 FF, a one pound box

And, sweetened condensed milk stocked in 1940! At 102 FF per can. Since the free sale of milk is getting nearer, the government liquidates its stock because it is afraid that the stock will remain unsold in perpetuity Overall, situation unchanged for the moment.

My first attempt at medical school lasted about one year. In those days, not only did you not pay, you were admitted if you had passed your pre-entrance Baccalauréate exams, the PCB. Unlike the American system, which rigorously weeds out unsuitable students before admission, the French system is open to all. However, and it's a giant however, try to stay in school. In addition to the lectures and lab classes, hospital work or stages were part of the schedule, even at the first-year level. At the end of the school year we were required to take both oral and written exams. Students who did not pass were allowed to repeat the year one time. I passed the first time, but again because of world events, I left medical school and took a detour.

Before I start the next part of this memoir, I have to mention one other little item.

"Daddy, are you going to talk about Eliane?" Charlotte and I looked at each other, puzzled by this question from our daughter Cecile. "Eliane, who?" we asked. We were still in the dark. Cecile soon set us straight. "Your first wife!"

This is probably news to most of our friends since I have never spent much time talking about it. Since Charlotte and I have been married for 50 years, it is an episode that truly happened a long time ago. However, there is no time like the present.

After I returned to Paris in early 1946, I met a young woman who, like me, had dreams of going to America. We dated for a while and when she became pregnant, I felt an obligation to marry her. I did not tell my parents; I'm not sure that anyone in the family knew about our marriage. I did know this was not a life that I wanted. Eliane's father paid the rent for a small apartment and for a short time we had some semblance of married life together. She miscarried not long after we were married. I'm sure I was relieved. I don't remember how she felt, but probably about the same. The marriage was over when I made the decision to go to Israel during the War for Independence. She had no interest in going to that region.

We lost track of each other. However, I did not bother to obtain a divorce. It was only at Mario's prodding years later that I asked him to make the necessary arrangements to finalize the divorce.

EIGHT

....

ISRAEL

As I mentioned in an earlier chapter, I was not brought up in a religious atmosphere although my family and I felt strongly about our Jewish heritage. We believed in the cause of the Jews. For nearly a century, our families had been accorded the same rights as those of the non-Jewish French citizens living in Algeria. Compared to the pogroms, inquisitions, and horrors that have beset Jews throughout the ages in other parts of the world, our lives were not threatened because of our religious heritage. Although there were unwelcome restrictions for Jews in North Africa during World War II, the hostilities and political situation did not have an impact on us as it did for millions of our fellow Jews in Europe.

After the war, the world attempted to come to grips with the effects of Nazi Germany's systematic extermination policies against Jews. World sympathy for their plight led the newly created United Nations to carve out a homeland for Jews in the area known as Palestine.

First some background; in the early 20th century, the breakup of the Ottoman Empire, of which Palestine had been part, created new countries as old ones were dissolved. This led to the partition of land and people in the Middle East. The British established a Mandate over Palestine, the Trans-Jordan area, and Iraq. The French, having taken over the goverenment of Algeria and Morocco 100 years earlier, claimed Lebanon and Syria as well. Egypt remained "independent," although the British maintained control until 1952.

In effect, these European powers created countries with artificial borders. This is where the trouble started—blending tribes with vastly different beliefs and allegiances. Virtually all were Muslims, yet the Arabs in the different areas had little in common apart from their religion. The Europeans maintained control over these newly formed countries through treaties, often among themselves, and maintained tight rules to keep the underlying differences from erupting into violence.

The situation changed at the end of the World War II. The era of colonization by the Europeans was ending quickly, but in many countries, with bloodshed. Independence from the British had already come to India in 1947; in the 1950s and '60s most of the colonies in Africa and Asia would revert to the control of the indigenous people of those countries.

Promises of independence for all these countries, except Algeria, had been made and broken many times and more than one agreement was made in secret. I won't delve any further into the complexities of the region. Let's recognize the same problems exist today with no resolution in sight.

We anticipated the United Nations' declaration of statehood for Israel. The actual date of independence, May 14, 1948, occurred as the last British troops left the country. Israel's Arab neighbors immediately declared war on the new state. This was a war Israel was ill equipped to fight; the Air Force, for example, had only eight planes. Although America and the Soviet Union recognized the State of Israel immediately, the U.S. also enforced a ban on the sale of arms to the country. You could say it was the U.S. arms embargo that led me into helping Israel.

My Jewish friends in Paris, including Maurice Bensimon, a friend from flight school, and I followed the news from the Middle East closely. Bensimon had given my name to an Israeli recruiter. About six weeks after hostilities started, I received a phone call asking if I would ferry an airplane to Israel. My expenses were to be reimbursed, but I was not paid. Like Bensimon, I held a French passport, so I could enter and leave a country.

Pilots with Israeli papers were not welcome in most European states. Since the U.S. arms embargo prevented arms sales, Israel-bound flights or pilots could not land in most European countries. Czechoslovakia was the sole exception to this prohibition. The country was the trading bazaar for the Israelis, who arranged for sales and deliveries of used planes and equipment from friendly sources in other countries to be transported to Israel.

The final destination was never noted on the bill of sale, the cargo, flight plans or logs. Transport routes for moving the vital war goods were devious and often involved long detours to avoid suspicion that the plane's final destination was Israel. In some countries, our plane was impounded when we arrived. We could do nothing but wait until Israeli agents arrived and secured a release for the plane.

I agreed to the caller's request. On June 29, 1948, I met Bensimon at an airport west of Paris, and we began our odyssey in a Norseman, a single-engine bush pilot plane. First, we flew to Bourges, a town in central France. After spending the night there, we went on to Nice, where we waited more than a week for clearance. Remember, we were traveling under false pretenses and could not tell the authorities at each airport the plane's ultimate destination. Finally, on July 11, Maurice and I were cleared to fly from Nice to Strasbourg. The following day we continued on to Zatek Airport, Brno, Czechoslovakia. My pilot logbooks show a mysterious lapse from the time of our arrival in Brno until I boarded a Pan Am flight four days later. However, for the only time in my logbook entries, the departure location is not listed. We landed in Brno five hours after we departed. As my memory has waned in the 60 plus years since that time, I believe I had taken off from Israel. There are no distances within the continental areas in which I was flying that would last five hours. I assume I did not want a record of landing or departing from Israel in my logbooks.

From Brno another pilot and I took a British-made Consul airplane to Ajaccio, Corsica. We left the plane, which had been purchased by the Israelis for another crew, to continue the trip back to the new country. For the final leg of this trip, we boarded an Air France flight in Ajaccio and returned to Paris.

In the fall of 1948 I resumed my medical studies, but eight months later in April 1949, I received another call from the same recruiter. This time, he asked me to fly to Nice to ferry a British-made, twin-engine Consul. The pilot was British and I was the copilot. Most of the legs required an overnight stop. It was not that we were dropping off and picking up cargo, we were simply attempting to cover our flight route. I think in reality the French knew what we were doing but looked the other way.

Our flight plan began in Nice on April 13 with a flight to Brindisi, Italy. From there we flew to the island of Rhodes. For our last stop that day, we continued towards Cyprus in a plane without navigational aids. We temporarily, and I want to stress this word, lost our way and missed Cyprus! It was night flying by sight and dead reckoning. We were able to locate Cyprus by doing a square search. What is a square search? Take a heading, perhaps north, fly in that direction for a certain number of minutes, say 15 minutes, then as the term implies, make a one-quarter turn, in this case from east or west and continue across the northern part of the square for another 15 minutes. Once you've reached that corner, either east or west, depending on which way you turned, make another one quarter turn and fly south. When you have flown 15 minutes, turn one more time in the opposite direction from which you flew the northern pattern. If you were paying attention, in one hour you will have flown a square. Somewhere in that square you will have found your destination, in our case, Cyprus. We landed safely, if a bit late. In those days and circumstances we weren't expected until we landed.

It was another week before we were allowed to leave Cyprus. Once given permission, we went directly to Tel Aviv's Lydda airport. From there, I flew back to Paris on a commercial flight.

Let me say something about this group of foreign recruits. We were part of what was known as the Machal, the Hebrew word for Overseas Volunteers. Not all were Jewish. It was a diverse group, made up of 4,400 men and women. Most were World War II veterans. Pilots, sailors, physicians, radio operators and mechanics from 56 countries came to help Israel, including many Americans. Four of us, including Maurice Bensimon and I, came from France.

I want to be clear: many overseas volunteers had a much more active and dangerous role than me. More than 100 from this group, including four women, lost their lives. I was one of the lucky ones.

There are a number of Web sites that offer a detailed history of the participants in the struggle for Israel's independence. www.machal.org.il is comprehensive, so detailed even my name is mentioned.

Below is an extract from this Website about the plane ferrying operation in which I was a participant:

> Fifty surplus US Army Norsemen were available for purchase in Europe. These planes were used extensively as transport aircraft during World War II, and would be particularly useful in supplying essential items to isolated kibbutzim in the Negev. In fact, the first three planes had already left Rome on May 2nd, 1948, and went into ser-

vice on the morning after their arrival in Israel, dropping supplies to the encircled Etzion Bloc."

"The Norsemen were sturdy Canadian aircraft designed for bush work. Somaco purchased twenty Norsemen, ostensibly for use in the Belgian Congo. All 20 aircraft were to be delivered in Rome by 1st June 1948, and five were delivered in late April."

"On May 29th, 1948, Canada's top World War II ace, George "Buzz" Beurling, together with well-known ex-RAF pilot Leonard Cohen, were practicing take-offs and landings at the Urbe Airport near Rome, in preparation for ferrying their Norsemen to Israel. Their plane caught fire in the air, and was engulfed in flames by the time it landed. Both died in the accident. Sabotage was suspected, but never proved."

"Three Norsemen, on their flight from Rome to Israel, were lost to the Egyptians. Flying in formation, they ran out of fuel in adverse weather conditions and had to force land in Sinai, with the crews ending up as prisoners-of-war. The crews were: American pilots Robert Daniel Fine, William Maldive, and Al Trop; Dutch pilot Victor Abraham

Wijnberg; and British navigator Hugh Curtiss."

"The six pilots who successfully reached Israel were Gino Narboni of France; Freddy Fredkins and Joe Sunderland, both British; and Americans Phil Marmelstein, Max Gordon, and Lou Lenart."

"On May 10th, on a mission to bomb Beit Machsir, a Norseman piloted by Israeli Yariv Sheinbaum crashed into the side of a hill near Saris. Together with him, co-pilot Daniel Burstein, radio operator Shlomo Cohen, bomb-chuckeers Itzhak Shakenowitz, Shlomo Rothstein and Zvi Shusterman, all Israelis, were killed."

"In June, the Norseman flights to Israel were discovered by David N. Miller, a former U.S. Army officer who worked as an aircraft broker in Paris. The U.S. embassy asked the French to ground all aircraft handled by Miller, and revoked his U.S. passport for any travel other than a direct return to the United States. All further deliveries of the planes from Germany were stopped. Therefore, as from 29th October 1948, only five Norsemen were operational in No. 35 Flight, based at Ekron (Tel Nof).

Six weeks after my previous flights, the Israelis contacted me again. This time they asked if I would move permanently to Israel and help build Israel's Air Force. It was a move I was ready to make. Medical school was put aside without any hesitation. I loved to fly and I wanted to help Israel.

This time, I took the train from Paris to Marseille. From there I boarded a ship to Haifa, Israel. I arrived in Israel in July 1949 and was assigned to a squadron based at Ekron a military airport near Tel Aviv. In those days there were few formalities. I don't remember signing any papers or being sworn in, but I was given a commission and reported to duty as Captain Narboni. At last I was an officer!

It was still a small Air Force. Many of us came from different countries. Again, because we held foreign passports, we could travel to places that would not accept pilots carrying only Israeli papers.

In 1948, the Jews, among the most ancient of Middle Eastern residents, finally had a country to call their own.

In 2012 I returned to Israel for the first time since I left in 1951. Everywhere I went, I was treated with great kindness and thanked profusely. Those of us who left our countries to support Israel during the War for Independence are recognized as an essential part of the struggle.

Most of the aviation infrastructure had to be built from the ground up. Now that I was an Israeli Air Force pilot, I had to learn to fly all the planes at Ekron Air Base. It sounds difficult, but for experienced pilots, most of this training can be accomplished with a check ride. The planes were all twin-engine. The inventory included a Consul, Harvard, Dakota, a DC-4, and the Commando, a DC-46. My job was to fly support missions for the Israeli Army, ferrying supplies and carrying paratroopers on their training missions. I also did formation flying for a fly pass. Later, I would be the one who did the transition training for new pilots. Here, I'd like to say a few words about the training that Maurice Bensimon and I had received during our U.S. flight school program. I think it was recognized around the flight lines that we had been well trained. I know we passed every check ride without difficulty.

The War for Independence ended with armistices being signed between Israel and its Arab neighbors in 1949. I remained as a Captain in the Israeli Air Force until May 1950, when I made the transition from the Air Force to civilian flying. With my commercial pilot license, I was qualified to carry passengers so I signed on to Arkia Airlines, a domestic airline that still exists. Notice I don't mention leaving the Air Force; again, I don't remember any formal separation of service—I just started flying for Arkia and El Al. At first I made daily runs between Eilat, a seaside city on the Red Sea and Lydda, the Tel Aviv airport for Arkia, but when I started flying international routes I worked for El Al. During the 18 months I stayed with El Al, we flew between Tel Aviv, Rome, Zurich, Vienna, Paris, London, Amsterdam, and Nairobi. I was the copilot for the DC-4 flights, a Skymaster four-engine plane, and the Constellation, also with four-engines. On the C-46, a twin-engine plane, I was the captain.

Once in a while, levity broke out. I was the copilot on a positioning trip, (taking an aircraft from one location to another without passengers) which included a stewardess among the seven-member crew. In the DC-4, the toilet was located in the tail of the plane. When the captain was notified the stewardess had gone into the bathroom, he pushed the stick or control column forward, raising the tail for a few seconds. Imagine that the plane was flying straight one minute and suddenly the nose dipped and the tail went up. It was a short maneuver, lasting no more than a few seconds, but anyone sitting in the plane's tail would not be happy. I want to stress this was not my idea, but I'm sure I thought it was amusing.

Any aircrew member will tell you an uneventful flight is the best kind of flight. There were just two stressful times—once with Arkia in a C-46, while we were in the landing pattern, my copilot grabbed the wrong lever and the engine shut down. For a few moments before I re-started the motor, the activity level in the cabin was charged. Also with El Al, and again in a C-46, we rolled partway off the taxiway, got stuck in the mud while land-ing in Istanbul and were towed to the gate. Embarassing, but not dangerous.

On another occasion, I was scheduled to be the third officer on a Tel Aviv-to-Rome night flight. It was a DC-4, a plane that carried a pilot and two copilots. Even though all three officers were qualified pilots, the most junior was the navigator. As we walked to the plane, the British captain turned to me and said, "Narboni, can you navigate?" Of course, I said yes. In reality, most of my navigating experience was limited to what I had learned in flight school. Hearing that news, after we climbed aboard the plane, the pilot went directly to his bunk. The copilot took over and I went to my desk to begin navi-gating. Our radio direction finder was straightforward: I had to crank up the radio frequency for the station. We needed three stations and at the point where the three stations intersected, we could find our present location. We continued flying and repeated the maneuver as we brought in new stations. No question, I was nervous. It had been a long time since I had been responsible for navigation, but we hit all the checkpoints, landing safely and on time.

Israel was, and remains today, the only democracy in the region. In 1951, the citizens were filled with hope for the future. For me, I found it crowded, populated with people who knew what they wanted, but for whom waiting was difficult. My only friends in Israel were Maurice and his wife. I was overwhelmed with the frenetic pace of life. I was not comfortable with the crowds nor with queuing up for every activity, so 18 months after the war ended, I returned to France with the intention of returning to medical school.

In reality, my goal was to return to the United States.

NINE

....

RETURN TO FRANCE
PART DEUX

In the fall of 1951 when I returned to France, I had already been involved in two conflicts. I was 28 years old, I could fly a plane and I was proficient in English; but I was still not sure where my skills and education would take me. My story was not unique; many in my generation had their lives changed forever because of World War II.

I didn't realize it at the time, but I would remain in France for only two more years. Today, as I look back on my career choices, I see many starts and multiple interruptions. The time I spent in Paris until my emigration to the United States in 1954 was a precursor to my ultimate goal to combine careers in medicine and aviation. How lucky I have been!

Life in Paris was still unsettled following the war. I had limited financial resources. My parents helped and supported my goal of returning to medical school. Yes,

this was attempt number two. Fortunately, I had passed
my exams during the previous stay so all I really had to
do was stand in one line after another until all the papers had been signed and stamped. Voila! I was again a
medical student at the University of Paris.

Correspondence with my parents gave them a sense
of my hard work and dedication. In this I was no
different from most students, who since the beginning
of time want their parents to know they are getting their
money's worth.

Rereading the letters I sent, I marvel at my own sense
of myself. In addition to being turgid, many of my letters
have a self-important air:

> I am overcome by the schedule which
> does not allow me time to write and even
> more ominously, the time to work. Since al-
> ready several days, I have to get up at 8 am
> to run to the hospital. The time for the care-
> free schedule is past. Now, they carry roll
> calls, conferences with slides and record-
> ings, patient presentations. A Chief of Ser-
> vice, the attending physician, is specifically
> in charge of the students. He does not leave
> even for one step, he assigns patients by
> beds, supervises the teaching of methods of
> auscultation, percussion, questioning of the
> patient, review of the cardio and radiologic

data at least twice a week. The Patron, also a physician of distinction, presents a conference on pathology and demonstrates auscultation of a typical patient. Shedding some light on the gallop and serenade of which make auscultation of the heart so delicate and obscure

In this last sentence, I'm offering my own poetic interpretation of the heart's rhythm. There's much more commentary in these letters, but I think you get the idea.

I also continued with the French Armée de l'Air reserves. The French armed forces, like military forces anywhere, provide an action-ready force in case of conflict, allowing members of the reserves to gain experience and maintain skills. For me, it meant I could continue to fly. My flight logs from 1953 indicate I flew frequently on training missions.

Wait a minute! I was just writing about the heavy burden of medical school life and now I'm going through my flying schedule?

I stayed in medical school for only one year after my return to France from Israel. I wonder what my parents must have thought.

In 1953, I applied for an immigrant visa for the U.S. My plan was to immigrate to America, then join the United States Air Force as a commissioned officer and continue flying! You can tell my life was unsettled. Yes, I was still married, but not living with my wife.

I was fortunate when I applied for a green card. I listed Algeria as my birthplace. This was one time when it was good luck to be born in that country because I was told I could apply under that country's quota. In the mid-'50s not many Algerians thought about moving to America. If I had been born in France, there would have been a longer wait for the visa.

While I waited for permission to settle in America, I found a job as the manager of the Post Exchange (PX) at the U.S. Army post in Orléans, a mid-size town about 80 miles from Paris. I knew I could improve my English skills by working for the Americans, but did not realize I would get on-the-job training in managing people. I can't say that I excelled in this endeavor. Most employees were foreigners, neither French nor Americans, but war refugees from the defeated Axis countries. They were known as DP's, short for displaced persons. Many, but not all, had been in Nazi concentration camps. For a period of time in the postwar era, western countries, including France and the U.S., agreed to help resettle them. I was dealing with unhappy employees who bickered among themselves on a daily basis even with their limited English and French language skills. They had lost everything except their lives. I didn't improve the situation; they resolved their differences themselves because they needed work to survive. At this, they were experts.

In early 1954 my immigration visa arrived. I was bound for America!

TEN

....

BEFORE I LEAVE PARIS, AGAIN

I've saved the most important influence in my life until now. This seems like an appropriate place to give credit where credit is due—to my family. My parents always stood by me, emotionally and financially. My father never gave up his dream that I would become a physician. I'm glad I was finally able to grant him this wish.

So much of the confusion over my Italian-sounding name, including my last name, comes because my mother gave us all Italian nicknames. She was born in Tunisia, a French protectorate that included a substantial Italian population. I became Gino, although my real name is Roger and Nathan, my Hebrew name. Family and friends address Mario by his Italian nickname, but professionally he uses Victor, his formal name. For some reason, Yvan, my youngest brother, never used his Italian nickname, Silvio.

Following the war, Mario, who had been drafted as an interpreter in Charles de Gaulle's Free French Forces, entered law school at the University of Paris. The regular army had been dissolved when France fell to the Germans in 1940. After the Liberation, the volunteer forces became the regular French Army.

Before I continue with Mario's career path, I'd like to write a few words about my uncle, Lucien Daninos, who was instrumental in helping Mario after he graduated from law school.

Lucien, a tenor, had a long and distinguished career at the Opéra Comique in Paris. According to his granddaughter Julia Daninos, an artist and *humoriste* in Paris:

> My grandfather sang 35 operas while at the Opéra Comique. He had the leading roles in Carmen, Tosca, Madam Butterfly, Faust, The Tales of Hoffman, *La Favorita* and many more.

> Lucien did not start his musical life without great effort. His father made him promise to complete law school before attempting to launch his musical career. In addition to his singing abilities, Lucien, an accomplished violinist, won first prize in violin at the Toulouse Conservatory. In spite of all these accomplishments, Lucien was a man of great simplicity.

When I grow up I want to be . . .

His wife, my grandmother, Marguerite
Bacri, was one of the great *"tragédienne "* or
dramatic actresses of the time and she
taught him how to interpret the various op-
eratic roles. It was for this reason that he
had such great success at the Opéra.

My own memories of Lucien come from my Aunt
Marguerite, who told me that life as a musician was difficult, often because of the attitude and jealousies among
the singers.

Lucien and Marguerite's apartment was in the 17th ar-
rondissement. The Avenue de la Grands Armée was a chic
address near the Champs Elysées. I assume like so many
musicians, Uncle Lucien retired with a modest pension.
When I saw him last in 1963, he and his daughter,
Monique, had started their own small business, renting
their chic address to business owners who did not have
access to such a fine location. They collected mail for the
address renters, took phone messages and transmitted
the letters and calls to the owners. No one had to wait in
line at Uncle Lucien's post office. In fact, according to
my cousin, Claude Bonan, "For more than 20 years my
uncle was the only one in France who offered this address rental service of *domiciliations des sociétés.* "He had
an enormous number of imitators, but unfortunately he
was never able to collect royalties for his idea."

At the time of Mario's graduation from law school, Lucien's son, Jean-Daniel Daninos, a film director and screenwriter, was making a movie in Italy, so Mario used the empty room and the address for his first office.

For Mario's next step up the career ladder, he rented an office on the Rue St. Denis. This street was in an area frequented by prostitutes. My brother, being a kind soul, said he would invite me to lunch whenever I came to his office. Naturally, a free invitation was not to be ignored, and as I was again a student in medical school with a limited budget, I took him at his word and frequently visited his Rue St. Denis office at lunchtime. There was an air of commerce along this street. The lineup of prostitutes, some of whom offered their services, was always there. Since I was a regular at Mario's office, I suspect they recognized me. Mario, at that stage in his career, frequently represented these ladies. As they paid for his legal assistance with cash, he never had to send an invoice.

From those humble beginnings, Mario moved to more elegant addresses, all of which had apartments attached to the office. Mario, now retired, had a long and successful career as a lawyer. Françoise, his late wife, practiced law with him for many years, and today their son, Pascal, carries on the family name in the law firm of Narboni et Associés.

When I grow up I want to be . . .

Like all the French Algerians, my brother Yvan and my sister-in-law, Arlette knew life would change after the referendum. In anticipation of the upheaval they moved to Toulouse, a city in the southwest part of France in 1962. Yvan taught school and Arlette, a pharmacist, owned and operated a pharmacy for more than 20 years. They still live in Toulouse, a charming city with ancient roots in French history. Their daughter, Caroline, a lawyer specializing in labor law, lives nearby.

Yvan, a gentle and kind soul, has a great interest in American films. He loves to quote movie dialogue. It's always fun to hear him mimic an American accent as he says his favorite lines, most of them from classic films.

My mother and her sisters were beautiful. That's not just a son's assessment. Charlotte confirms this, as she believed her mother-in-law remained beautiful her entire life. However, my mother came not only from an earlier generation, but also from a vastly different culture. No doubt because of her background and upbringing, Aurette had a special way of looking at the world. At the beginning of our marriage, Charlotte had reservations about their relationship, a mutual feeling on my mother's part. It took about 10 years for Aurette and Charlotte to realize each other's worth. Fortunately, time solved the differences in their approaches to life and they became good friends with mutual feelings of love and respect.

Aurette told fantastic stories. So fantastic, many were unbelievable. However, there was always a grain of truth buried in each tale. You had to be careful about dismissing her words because you would eventually learn at least one portion of her assessment or story was correct.

One of my favorites involved Aurette attempting to pass through U.S. customs carrying a suitcase filled with fresh, smelly cheeses and, *saucission,* or salami. It was the early '80s; we were living in San Antonio and had driven 200 miles to Houston to take my mother to our home. As she spoke no English, it would have been too difficult for her to change planes on the East coast. She knew, of course, that food could be confiscated, so she locked the suitcase and tucked away the key. When asked to see its contents at customs, she refused to open it. Aurette did not understand the English request but she certainly understood the intent. As you know, no one is allowed behind the customs barrier. On this occasion, the rules were bent. We were waiting outside the doors, wondering why it was taking so long since the other passengers had departed. Eventually, an agent came to the door and asked, "Is there a Colonel Narboni here?" My mother never tired of telling people her son was a doctor and a colonel! They escorted me into the restricted area so I could translate for them. When I arrived, I could see a female customs officer crying. Hmm . . . At this point, the officials just wanted to be certain Aurette was being met in the U.S. They no longer insisted she open the suitcase. I want to emphasize Aurette was never rude or mean so I assume they just couldn't deal with her any longer. She had told them the key didn't work and refused to budge, either in changing her story or surrendering the key.

Mother was a wonderful cook. She had at her fingertips, the best produce, cheeses, meats and fish for which France was famous. Everything to eat was as close as the nearest *marché* and the small shops that surrounded her home in Constantine and later her apartment in Paris. Even if her cupboard was bare she could create memorable meals with just a few ingredients from the pantry or from her small, utilitarian refrigerator. Soup was one of her specialties. That doesn't sound particularly inspiring, but my mother could take a bone, some water, spices, a vegetable or two and end up with a rich, flavorful base on which to build a consommé, stock, bisque, or broth. My father, who was extremely fussy and did not like or was "allergic" to eggs, cream, cheese, and butter, nevertheless was given some or all of these items in one form or another each day. Georges was frail and his health precarious, so Aurette spent time and effort attempting to enrich his diet. No talk of cholesterol and high fat foods in those days!

All her life, Aurette maintained lively and voluminous written correspondence with her sisters and cousins, including those who lived in far-flung parts of France and Tunisia. Since I always seemed to be in a foreign land, my mother also wrote long, descriptive letters to me. A cousin described Aurette's role in the family as the family chronicler. This was an important role, and, at the time not completely understood or appreciated by me. Each letter she wrote gave the latest information about the health, marital state, and fantastic progress of all the family members. It was a bit like Camelot; it only rained at night. In our family, success was guaranteed for those with the last name of Narboni, Daninos, etc. Charlotte said no one ever failed or had shortcomings, that is, unless they had not been born into the family, but had instead just married one of those perfect relatives.

The political situation in Algeria during my final medical school years was worsening. There were calls from several factions, including the indigenous Arab population, for France to grant Algeria its independence. Fighting to force the French to give up control had started in 1954 and continued for the next eight years. In 1958, Charles de Gaulle was reelected because the voters felt he was the only one who could bring the armed rebellion to a successful conclusion. For the French that meant Algeria would remain under French control. Even after De Gaulle's election, the bloody conflicts continued with violence on both sides, those who wanted independence from France as well as a strong faction in the French army that insisted Algeria remain French. The end came in September 1959 when De Gaulle reversed his earlier, pre-election, no separation for Algeria position and argued for independence. The issue was subsequently settled by referendum in Algeria. In 1962, a nearly unanimous vote signaled the end of French control of Algeria.

Life for the French changed overnight. Although, technically, it was possible to stay in Algeria, life and property for the French were threatened. With the Algerians in charge, the French social system was no longer valid.

Our parents were well into middle age when the conflict began in 1954. As Gaullistes, they had believed in General de Gaulle since 1940. He could not do this to them. They wanted to remain in Constantine.

After the referendum and a date for independence was set, my parents knew it was time to go. They were the last family members to leave Algeria. Members of the younger generation who could start again in France had departed earlier to establish a new life. Many, like Mario, never returned to Algeria after the war.

My brother found an Arab buyer for the Sidi Mabrouk house and the final sale price, a fraction of its value, was arranged. French citizens who left Algeria were not allowed to take money or property out of the country, but thanks to Mario, the transaction was successfully concluded in France. He also helped our parents find an apartment in a Paris suburb, which they bought with their savings and the proceeds from the sale of the house.

There is one final note on my parents' departure from Algeria. In 1964, after they moved to Paris, when Charles de Gaulle's name was mentioned, my father and mother always made negative comments. However, when General de Gaulle passed away in 1971, my mother wrote to me and expressed her sadness. After all those years of vituperation about his role in the loss of their homeland, she was still willing to recognize the many good deeds Charles de Gaulle had accomplished for France.

I think the French who were born and raised in that beautiful land would have accepted the transition for Algeria's independence if they had been given more time to adapt to the changing situation. In their defense, the French believed Algeria was part of France. They felt they were evicted from their homeland.

ELEVEN

....

UP, UP, AND AWAY

In 1954, I found myself on a ship bound for America. This time, I wasn't sharing a cabin with seven other 22-year olds. However, my accommodations were far from luxurious; I had an inside room without a porthole, buried deep in the heart of the *Ile de France*, one of the great ocean liners of the time.

I was assigned at a table for eight in the restaurant serving tourist-class passengers. Even in this section of the ship, the food was acceptable. As I had already spent time in the U.S., I had a well-formed opinion about American dietary habits. Then, we were under wartime restrictions, but I carried a typical French sense of superiority about food served anywhere but on French soil. Tourist-class meals aboard the *Ile de France* qualified as part of France. At dinner, one evening, I watched as an American seated at my table added a couple of teaspoons of sugar to her glass of red wine. I thought to myself, is this what I can expect from life in America?

After we docked in New York, I had to undergo a physical exam as part of the immigration process. When questioned about my parents' health, I mentioned my mother's stay in a TB sanitarium, so I had to have a chest x-ray before I was cleared for entrance into the U.S.

Once the process was finally completed, I took my bags and embarked on another 1950s uniquely American experience. I checked into a YMCA, basing this decision on my financial resources. I had come to the US with $500, my life savings, and I did not have any idea how long I would have to be on the streets.

I had a plan. I was going to join the United States Air Force. I was going to fly! I had my visa; I would become an American. My first stop towards achieving this goal took me to a recruiting station in Battery Park, near the southern tip of Manhattan.

I showed up with my documentation, my pilot wings, immigration papers, and other evidence proving I was a legitimate officer candidate.

There was just one component missing. I was not an American citizen. The recruiter explained that I would have to become a naturalized citizen before I could be an officer. At that time, and even today, the rule, which had expired, was reinstated for the Afghanistan and Iraq conflicts. A legal non-citizen serving in the armed forces could become a citizen in six months. I'm not sure if I heard the whole spiel correctly, but I was told that after completing the naturalization process, I could apply for Officer Candidate School (OCS), become an officer and by extension, a pilot!

At least, that's what I believed. I raised my right hand, pledged my allegiance to the Constitution of the United States and became Airman Basic Gino Narboni. Here I was at the age of 31, starting down yet another career path.

A short time later I joined a group of recruits, who like me, were headed for basic training. We boarded a bus for Sampson Air Force Base, one of two USAF basic training installations. The base was on the shores of Seneca Lake, one of New York's beautiful Finger Lakes. (Two years later, in 1956, it was closed. Since that time, all enlisted USAF personnel attend the basic training course at Lackland AFB in San Antonio, Texas.)

Basic training is pretty much the same in any military situation. You learn the rules, how and when to salute, to march, and to follow orders. It's not exciting, but it provides the foundation for turning men and women into a cohesive unit capable of completing a mission. Since my goal was to obtain my citizenship within six months, I believed basic training was just one extra step to take before I could go through OCS, the USAF's Officer Candidate School. It did not bother me that I had to go to the process again even though this was my fourth time as a recruit. As the French say, *Je connais la chanson*—I know the song.

Since I had military experience, I was given the responsibility as a flight leader. In this situation, flight had nothing to do with flying. I served as the point person to keep the group in order when marching. Basic training was unremarkable except for one memorable moment. Our flight 3335 (I still have the flag with the number) was standing at attention in parade formation. As flight leader, I was in the front of the group. Even though I was an Airman Basic, I was entitled to wear my pilot wings, probably the only enlisted man in the United States Air Force with this privilege.

At these parades, an officer reviews the troops, checking on the quality and discipline of the formation. The officer in charge, a major, reviewed our flight. As he passed in front of me, he stopped, looked at the pilot wings pinned to my shirt and said, "I don't know what you did, but it must have been bad to be busted so low!" I've never forgotten this moment. He assumed I had been an officer but had gotten into so much trouble I had been stripped of my rank and reduced to the very lowest rung on the USAF ladder. Being the flight leader I knew a reply was not expected or wanted, but I'll bet he could not come up with an answer. He probably told his version of this story as many times as I've told mine.

When I grow up I want to be . . .

After 11 weeks of basic training at Sampson, we were sent to our next assignment. As a foreign national, I did not have a security clearance so I was not eligible for specialized or advanced training. Instead, I was sent to another upstate New York installation. This time, the stop was Watertown, a small radar station on the St. Lawrence River. My arrival coincided with the beginning of a long, bitterly cold, snowy winter.

I was assigned as a clerk in the Morale, Recreation, and Welfare section. In a remote assignment like Water-town, the MRW was a popular department with the troops. It had a lending library and a storeroom stocked with sports equipment. My job was to stamp the books and sign out basketballs and skis. As an extra bit of daily spice, I listened to music, playing selections from a stack of classical music 78's I found in the back room. Since I controlled the needle, I played what I liked.

In Watertown, everyone was looking for entertain-ment, particularly for activities to fill the long winter evenings. To help with the boredom, my unit organized the evening social programs, which included a French Club and an adult band. The local high school music teacher served as the conductor. He was also active in the French Club, for which I was the unofficial advisor. Here, we had mutual interests. He offered me a spot in his band in exchange for helping him with French les-sons. Like any young man, I headed for the percussion section and the snare drums. Unfortunately, I can't read music, so I relied on my natural sense of rhythm to carry me through. I'm not sure how good I was, but I do remember he laughed every time I played.

Eventually, the big day arrived. On November 5, 1954, nearly six months from the date of my application, I became a naturalized citizen of the United States. I am as proud today as I was when I took the oath. Although a new citizen of the United States, I remain a French citizen. It is guaranteed for life. Since the time of Napoleon, all French males shall remain French unless stripped of it for treason. "Born French, die French."

What was I thinking? I paid a visit to the USAF personnel office the day after I became a citizen. There I learned the truth, that I could not be accepted as an officer candidate. I would not be going to Officer Candidate School. As the Korean War hostilities had ended, additional pilots were not needed so there were no direct commission slots available. Only medical officers and chaplains could receive a commission without graduating from a service school such as West Point or the Naval Academy.

I had no option other than to finish the remaining three years of my four-year enlistment. I've never been one to rail against perceived injustices or inequalities or even my own less-than-brilliant decisions, so I said to myself, "I still want to be around planes." And, I wanted to return to Europe.

The Air Force treated me well even though I was not an officer. In the four years I served in the enlisted ranks, I was recognized as a special case because I was a commissioned pilot with a university education.

Now that I was a citizen and eligible for advanced training, I asked to go through the Aircraft Engine Mechanic School. This would keep me on the flight line. Within a month, I was sent to the training course at Chanute Air Force Base, Rantoul, Illinois. Again, I was placed in an accelerated program, and within a couple of months I passed the final exam!

With my aircraft engine mechanic certificate in hand, I was assigned to Rhein Main Air Force Base in Germany, a transport facility attached to the Frankfurt International Airport. These facilities have since been turned over to the Germans and are now part of the civilian commercial airport.

In 1955, Germany was still very much in the postwar period with frequent food and fuel shortages. As Americans, we were protected since we had access to U.S. goods and low-cost gas for our cars at the Base Exchange facilities.

Base living conditions were another story. By now, I had been promoted to Airman First Class. I'm sure I could have lived on the economy, but I stayed in base quarters. For airmen of my rank, the living quarters were open bays. Here I was, 30 years old, still sharing sleeping quarters with 20 other men, most in their early '20s. Naturally, the bathroom facilities were down the hall. I tell this story to Charlotte, who cannot understand how someone my age could spend three years living in these conditions.

Let me say a word or two about my job as an aircraft engine mechanic. I may have helped repair the occasional airplane engine, but in reality, I drove a Coleman Tractor. This is the truck used to tow airplanes after they land and before they take off. Rhein Main, which served as the gateway for most U.S. armed forces stationed in Germany, ran a 24-hour operation with planes arriving and departing around the clock. We worked 12-hour shifts, winter and summer. Outdoor jobs have shortcomings. The winters were so cold we could not stay outside more than 30 minutes at a time. If it wasn't snowing, it rained.

I was the first ground crew member to board a plane after the pilots and passengers had gone. My job was to perform a minor interior system check before the plane left on its next flight. I increased my English skills from reading the discarded magazines I picked up on these forays.

One day, a friend and I showed up late for work. Our sergeant, who was not happy, made us wash an airplane as punishment! It was not as awful as it sounds even though it was a large, four-engine DC-6. We used a high-pressure hose and accomplished our job in about an hour. After that experience, we managed to get to work on time.

I enjoyed my time as an enlisted man. By the end of my third year I was promoted to staff sergeant. To make this rank within 36 months is not an easy task, but again, I was older, experienced and responsible, apart from the airplane-washing incident.

Now that I was a sergeant, I became a dispatcher. This meant I could stay inside. No more time spent outdoors in the bitter cold and the rain that never seemed to stop.

Being in Germany also meant that I could see my parents more often. They came each summer from Algeria to visit relatives and to spend time in France. My mother was in charge of finding accommodations. She seldom planned in advance, believing that we would always find a place to stay. I remember one episode in particular: I drove my Opel Kadett to Paris, picked up my parents and my brother Mario. From there, we drove to the South of France. Once there, we stopped for lunch in Vallauris, a lovely Provençal town tucked away in the hills above the Mediterranean Sea. A waiter who overheard us discussing our need for a place to stay told us his cousin had a vacation house for rent. We did not look at the house before paying for it. Yes, it was in a beautiful setting on a hilltop. It seemed perfect, but there was one amenity lacking, no indoor plumbing. Who would believe even budget accommodations along the Riviera would not have toilets?

To recap: I had been a recruit four times in four different military organizations; I had completed three years of medical school and I was still married, or in reality, not divorced. I was a pilot, but I was sleeping in the barracks and living a very frugal existence.

By now, the year was 1958; my four-year enlistment was nearly complete. What would or should I do?

One event finally pushed me into making a decision that would change my life.

In those days, Germany was still under postwar obligations. Probably to prevent the black market sale of U.S. currency, we were paid every two weeks in scrip we could exchange for Deutschmarks or dollars. On payday, a room in our unit was set up with a long table. The officers formed a queue on one side and enlisted personnel lined up on the other side. It was all in the open. We approached the table, showed the paymaster our ID cards and he counted out our pay, bill by bill. The same procedure was used for the officers' line. I realized it took much longer to distribute the stack of bills on the opposite side than the time needed to count out my small pile. Finally, I made the connection. I said to myself, "Enough Gino, time to get serious."

I completed my enlistment, requested separation from active duty in Germany, and made plans to return to Paris. This time when I asked for reinstatement at the medical school, I had the G.I. Bill, a program set up after World War II to help returning servicemen and women get an education. With the G.I. Bill, the U.S. government paid for expenses connected to my schooling. What a concept! Even more important, I would not be asking my parents for money any longer.

So, back to Paris and the Maison Belge one more time.

TWELVE

....

PARIS, MEDICAL SCHOOL, AGAIN

In today's world, it is difficult to believe I could start, stop, start, interrupt, and restart medical school for a third time. But, that's exactly what I did. I suspect the effects of World War II created temporary and artificial rules and regulations that would not be allowed today.

This time, I knew what I wanted; I was old enough and had enough experience on the lower employment rungs to know I could and should achieve larger goals. I'm sure my parents were pleased. They had supported me in all my earlier efforts, both with funding and encouragement.

My road map to becoming a physician was set; I just had to follow it. I had inquired about the rules for obtaining an internship in America. For me, they were simple. I would have to pass the English proficiency exam, the ECFMG, required of all foreign national physicians before they can enter the U.S. for training or practice. That, obviously, was not a problem. I would also have to complete a one-year internship in an accredited hospital program before I could obtain a license to practice medicine.

With these goals in mind, I returned to my studies; determined to graduate in as short a time as possible. The French medical school system requires six years to obtain a degree. The first five years, of which I had completed four, were devoted to classes and some patient care. The fifth year, which I was about to start, would be concentrated in pediatrics, surgery, medicine, obstetrics and psychiatry. Each required a stage in a different Paris hospital. The internship was counted as the final, or sixth year and a thesis, written and defended before a committee, was part of the graduation process. Finally, I had a plan.

Medical school is always demanding; there is more work and study than one could think possible. This time, while I don't want to say that I sailed through the program, I passed my classes without difficulty.

For my final medical school stay, I moved back to my old dorm, the Maison Belge. The room cost included the cleaning services of Madame Moquereau, a *femme de chambre*. Although we became friends, I never addressed her by her first name. She was probably in her '50s when I met her, a monument to sturdiness and a wonderful example of French determination. We kept in touch for many years, long after she had retired. Each winter she prepared large glass jars of *confiture de marrons*, or chestnut jam, prepared from the fall harvest. She boiled and peeled the chestnuts, then simmered them in sugar syrup perfumed with a vanilla bean. As the final step, Mme Moquereau pressed the chestnut mixture through a sieve until it became a smooth, thick purée. I bought several jars and kept them cool on my windowsill. A spoonful or two of chestnut jam scooped directly from the container always made studying more pleasant. Ask me today if I would prefer to have some fine caviar, which I do enjoy, or a jar of Madame Moquereau's chestnut jam? It wouldn't be a contest. Confiture de marrons would win every time!

Mme Moquereau was married to a bus ticket-taker. On board, passengers gave Monsieur Moquereau, or one of his colleagues, their tickets to be punched. No one who rides a public bus or Metro train discards the punched ticket before reaching the final destination. I have seen Metro police waiting at station exits, asking passengers to see the stub. There's a substantial fine, payable on the spot, for those who can't find the proof.

The same ticket system exists today, but instead of handing it over to a human, you insert the ticket in a machine that clicks to note your fare has registered and you are good to go. There's a ritual among some riders, particularly students, who are adept at climbing onto the bus through the rear door to avoid paying for the ride. Ask Cecile about this technique.

There was another feature of Paris trains and buses that existed in my time. A sign printed above two choice seats closest to the door of both Metro trains and the buses noted these seats were "*Réservé pour les femmes enceintes, les persons agés, et les Grands Blessés de la Guerre Mondiale.*' No one could sit in these special seats except pregnant women, elderly persons, or severely wounded soldiers from WWI. In France, the major battles during this conflict were fought within French borders and those who had participated in the conflict were regarded as deserving of honor and special consideration. My mother always used a version of this statement if there was an imagined or real slight against Georges or her: "*Ton père était un grand blessé de guerre!*" . . . Your father was badly wounded in the war! Everyone knew what she meant.

We visited Mme Moquereau at her home while we were living in Germany. By 1971, she had retired when my mother, Charlotte and I stopped to say hello on our way to a New Year's Eve dinner. The Moquereaus lived in Gentilly, a modest Paris neighborhood. Their small apartment was in the rear of the building, accessible only through a courtyard. Another couple was there and the four were preparing to celebrate the arrival of the New Year. In spite of the modest surroundings, Mme

Moquereau had a bottle of champagne cooling in a bucket and insisted we share a glass with them. A plate of hors' d'oeuvres placed carefully on a tray would start their special holiday celebration, and would be followed by dinner. In France, proper meals still counted as an essential part of life. My point in recounting this story from 40 years ago is that in just about any situation, the French can adapt and present whatever they have in a careful, caring manner. Vive la France!

Mario had introduced me to Charles Benamon, another character in my parade of friends and acquaintances. Like my family, Charles was from Algeria. When he settled in France, he carved out a successful business as a jute merchant buying and selling burlap sacks. Where did I fit in? Although, Charles hated to drive, he had a large, late-model, luxurious Citroën so I was happy to act as his chauffeur. When I had free time, we'd drive into the country, stop at farms and ask to buy old sacks, which Charles then sold to millers who used them to pack their grain and flour. I wasn't paid for this driving; I just enjoyed it. Charles liked to speed and he constantly yelled at me to go faster. One day, the inevitable happened. We were stopped. Fortunately, we didn't get a ticket because Charles convinced the gendarme we would drive more slowly in the future.

There were other jobs as well, mostly unpaid. My friends and cousins had been good to me for many years so it was natural to help them when I could. I babysat her son, Claude, for my cousin Josette. Now, Claude and his wife, Isabelle, are grandparents. Time passes quickly.

When I wasn't babysitting or chauffeuring, I assisted a general surgeon in the operating room. Mostly, I was there, scrubbed in, to hold the retractors and occasionally help tie a knot. This was interesting work because I thought I wanted to be a surgeon.

THIRTEEN

....

BACK TO AMERICA,
AGAIN

By 1960, I had traversed the Atlantic at least five times, but this crossing marked the beginning of my professional medical career.

To take the next step, I decided to apply to several hospitals and choose the first one that answered positively.

How little did I know the letter offering me an internship at the Deaconess Hospital in Buffalo, New York, would change my life! It was here that I met Charlotte Smith.

I arrived late, two months after the normal July start for interns, and according to Charlotte, who was a student nurse; I created a stir in the nursing school ranks.

Life in a hospital was different in those days; the lines and hierarchy were well defined and seldom breached. At the top were the Chiefs of Service for the different areas: surgical, medical and obstetrics. The

Chief Resident of each department was next in command followed by the residents and at the bottom of the ladder, the interns. Yes, again, I was at the lowest rung, but I had several advantages. I spoke English extremely well, unlike some of my fellow interns; I was older, and most importantly, I was French!

On the nursing side, there was an equally well-defined ladder, at the top of which was the Director of Nursing, then the Head Nurse on each floor, followed by the registered nurses, and below, the student nurses. This last group was also divided by year, so the youngest or first-year student ranked even below the interns. Charlotte was in her third and last year, so she had a certain level of superiority, or at least that's what she thought.

Charlotte will tell you the first time she saw me she decided I was the one!!! I admit I did not have the same feelings when I met her. I probably didn't think about her other than she was a female and all females have a special place in my thinking. Charlotte loves to tell the stories about me at the Deaconess; how I dated every nurse, both graduate and student, and I got around to her only as I neared the end of my one-year stay there.

She's not wrong; we had several meetings, none particularly memorable. Charlotte never tires of telling the story of how we met. Apparently, there was a patient who had to have his IV restarted. In those days, an intern did this procedure and a student nurse always accompanied him. The man had poor veins so it took about 30 minutes to find one. This meant the remaining veins in his arms were temporarily "shut down." At the end of this labor, after Charlotte and I had left the room, she remarked, "That certainly was a Pyrrhic victory." She says, but truly I don't remember, that I was surprised to learn a product of an American school would understand a Pyrrhic victory.

On another occasion, one of her classmates, whom I was seeing at that time, told me Charlotte played tennis. According to Charlotte, I informed her all my friends were busy or on call, which left her. "Would she play tennis with me?" Not exactly the romantic. She was wrong. Charlotte might have known how to hold a racket but her tennis ability was minimal.

Our next meeting occurred the night before her graduation. Again, I leave Charlotte to recount my enchanting patter. "We were at our favorite hangout, dancing and drinking beer. Gino asked me if I wanted to dance and after some time, said, 'I'm going for a drive; you can come along if you'd like.'" Ah, romance!

This was the beginning. In September 1961, I returned to Paris to submit my thesis. Now my letters from Paris were written to Charlotte instead of my parents. I was still full of myself.

Since arrival, I have been longing for a minute to simply sit down! No pity! School, relatives, friends, go, go, go. This means mainly walking, since traffic is so heavy, and the weather is so nice. On the brighter side, I have returned to my wine and my steak-French fries diet, a man's diet! And, by the way, 1961 seems to be a very good girl's vintage year in Paris. They are so sprightly, youthful, sexily dressed as I ever remember! Or is it just an impression, after a year of severe dieting? Whatever the reason, let's enjoy it while here, which will not be too long. The school has accepted, it seems, our position of particular hurriedness. We might be allowed (there are three of us) to speed up proceedings to the point where 4-6 weeks will see our return to the hamburger and sundaes paradise. I have returned to my old campus house, large, immortal amid the lawns and trees; everybody gladly extends a hand. "Monsieur Narboni! De retour parmi nous!" Et oui, Monsieur Narboni est une fois de plus à Paris." Once more in Paris, a city deeply liked, but to which I do not belong.

When I grow up I want to be . . .

Beautiful shops, deafening traffic, rivers of light, majestic stones, horde of fast-walking people, aimed like arrows at your back, resplendent cars, resplendent faces, pairs and pairs and pairs of swiftly-muscled legs, below swiftly flowing skirts, words, a ten feet thickness of words, you cut through, harsh words, insulting words, tender words, bellowing words.

World of words, noise, flesh, light, step on my toes, pinch my heart, awaken my desires, quench my thirst, assuage me, dazzle me, bully me. Run, run, run! Ouf!

Enough of everything offered, proffered, but nobody wants everything! Believe me, walks in the woods, moments of silence, dreams and solitude!

Dear Charlotte, friend last met and best liked of a sweetly dullish year of my life, please find in these lines, amity, compassion, hopes and wishes for you and me.

Devotedly, Gino

As I mention in my letter to Charlotte, I returned to the states without delay. My ultimate goal was to combine my love of flying with my newly minted status as a physician. I was accepted for the flight surgeon Primary Course training program at the School of Aerospace

133

Medicine, beginning October 1962. Do not confuse the word surgeon with a physician who operates. Surgeon is a designation used universally in the Armed Forces, with titles that range from Command Surgeon, the military physician in charge of medical affairs for multiple bases with the same missions, to Flight Surgeon, the physician who oversees the health of the flying personnel at an individual base.

I had nine months until school started, so I worked as a resident physician at a Long Island hospital. It was a busy time, as I noted in a letter to Charlotte, who by now, had graduated, taken her state boards and worked in a physician's office in Buffalo.

"Tonight I had supper prepared with my own soft hands; eggs, salami, cheese, salad, WINE, while a soft twisting music was playing. Afterward, a glass of sherry and my pipe in hand (very gentleman farmer) and to the sound of Beethoven 3rd *Marche Funèbre* proceed to enjoy a well-deserved digestion."

No question. The next and most important phase of my life was about to begin. One word says it all— Charlotte, or as our friends note I always say, "Char-Lotte" à la française.

Charlotte and four friends moved to New York in February 1962. They lived in an apartment hotel on West 110th Street off Broadway, an area still awaiting its renaissance. Time and distance where love is concerned do not matter. We continued to see each other as often as possible given our different schedules. By late summer, 1962, we were starting to skirt around talk of marriage. Nothing defined, just the occasional mention of a life together that would have to be planned since I still had one more school to attend.

The three-month Aviation Medicine program was located at Brooks Air Force Base, San Antonio, Texas. I had even been promised an assignment at a USAF base in England, giving me a chance to go back to Europe again. As I look back at my life now, I always seemed to want to be on the other side of the Atlantic, no matter whether it was in the U.S. or in Europe.

I'm not sure why, but I made the decision to get married. Remember, I had taken many years to finally end my previous marriage and I was somewhat reluctant to go down that path again. Here I was 38 years old, still in school, still living in university or hospital housing and still waiting for my real career to begin.

I'm going to let Charlotte give you her version of my proposal. She has repeated this story so often that it would be unfair to not give her the opportunity to tell it one more time.

One afternoon, Gino called me at my Manhattan apartment. He told me he had received a letter from his mother that day. I thought, 'that's nice.' Then, he mentioned he had written to tell her that he had met a girl, but there were several significant differences—age, religion, and culture. He was Jewish, I was not; he was 16 years older than me. I came from a rural background in Lancaster County, the heart of the Pennsylvania Dutch country. I will readily admit I was not sophisticated, but I loved Gino and nothing would have made me happier than to marry him.

I waited for Gino to continue with his mother's response. According to Gino, she said she was sure Gino would choose an outstanding person and she would welcome any woman to the family that Gino selected. So, Gino said, "I'm going to Flight Surgeon school for three months; I'll return In December and then we can get married." As an afterthought, he added, "If that's okay with you."

So much for romantic proposals! In spite of his tendency to tell me his decision before he asked for mine, I said yes, immediately. I have never regretted it.

That little chore taken care of, I left for Brooks Air Force Base, San Antonio, Texas, to begin my Air Force

career as an officer and physician. But, once again, I was
writing from a military facility:

1 October 1962

My beloved,

First day, a lot of paperwork, a lot of fast
work, bus rides, advice from a major-mentor,
processing, (What is your Father's name?
What is the color of your eyes?) There will
be more, much more of the same since the
real course starts only in two weeks and
lasts nine weeks. There will be course and
lectures on military etiquette, parades, uniforms, traditions; in brief, a big bundle of
light stuff to be polite. Again, I am in a batch
of youngsters, just out of internships; born
in 1936, and the like, but well behaved, ties
and coats worn at all times, quiet, probably
well tried and tired by years of meager in-
come. The one who shares my suite, (indeed
we are one to a room, but share small studio
with desk.) Very nice, but hopelessly young,
married, *bien sûr*, and one kid, *bien sûr, aussi.*
Arrived here with not a cent in his pocket.

We went to Lackland Air Force Base today, and I saw with nostalgia the basic airmen going through their paces, shaven head,
sweaty fatigues, coarse looks, farm boys or

city sleek, all cut to government size, and ponderously squashing the grass with their size 11's. 1954! I was one of them! 1962, I look at the captain's bars I just bought! Some progress, everything comes to those who wait and want!"

My barracks are on the edge of the flying field, the runway is not 200 yards away. By the way, meals are taken at the Officers Club, which means steak twice a day! They have nothing else. I can see this life, becoming pretty quickly super-organized, routine. That is why one needs a little wife to keep the curiosity going!

Je t'embrasse aussi fort que j't'aime. Gino

On another occasion, I wrote,

Here I am, starting my main job, all sails spread out, and a brisk force 3 wind blowing . . . I am not going to elaborate copiously since it is 9:30 pm, that I have quite a bit of reading and I want lights out by 11. Up by 7 am, that is a flat 8 hours . . . just enough!

It may have still been a job on the lower rung of the ladder, but I was on my way.

I shall tell you that indeed, after I completed the Aerospace Medicine Flight Surgeon course at Brooks AFB, I flew to Charlotte's home in Lancaster, Pennsylvania. Na-

When I grow up I want to be ...

than Roger Gino Narboni and Charlotte Anna Smith
were married at a small ceremony on December 20, 1962.

We had no time or money to spare for a honeymoon.
I had to report to my first assignment, Edwards Air
Force Base, by the end of the year.

FOURTEEN

....

CALIFORNIA, HERE WE COME!

PART I
EDWARDS AIR FORCE BASE
1962-1965

No more footloose and fancy free; that may not be a French expression, but I certainly understood the meaning! I had marked my 39th birthday while at Brooks Air Force Base. Now I was again embarking on a new career in an unfamiliar environment; most importantly, I had a new wife. I think if I thought about my situation, I would have been apprehensive. Maybe I didn't express it just like that, but there were challenges in my—excuse me—our new life.

I was due to report to Edwards by the end of December 1962. Neither Charlotte nor I had ever been in the western part of the States, so this trip to California was new for both of us. We were driving my 1958 white Chevrolet Bel Air I had bought in Buffalo two years earlier.

On Christmas Eve we crossed the Pecos Mountains in West Texas. Two days later we arrived at the California border and drove north until we arrived at Edwards. I should say we passed a large sign in the middle of nowhere that said, "WELCOME TO EDWARDS AIR FORCE BASE." All we could see was tumbleweed, sand, rocks, telephone poles, and the occasional stunted tree that looked dead. We learned later this was a Joshua tree and no, it wasn't dead. After about 15-18 miles of this terrain, we saw the first signs of life. Low buildings, planes, hangars, and in the distance, green, leafy trees marking the housing area.

I had been in multiple military outfits so I knew the routine: find the personnel office, always the first stop to sign in for a new assignment. It was still 1962—no cell phones and no computers; everything was handwritten or pecked on a typewriter. I now discovered the special attention given to officers, particularly those in the medical corps. We were welcomed warmly by the other flight surgeon with whom I would share responsibilities. But, for Charlotte, the housing officer was the most important person who came to greet us.

If you talk with military families, you will probably hear stories about how they had to wait months, if not years, for base housing. Base housing, as opposed to that in a town, is considerably less costly. The cost, based strictly on rank, is deducted from your monthly pay. As

Edwards was so isolated, virtually every married officer and most enlisted personnel were assigned to housing on the installation. No one in our memory ever moved in the day of arrival!

We were offered a modern three-bedroom, two-bath house on a tree-lined street. As we had only our luggage, moving in wasn't difficult. Because of its remote location, furniture and basic kitchen equipment were also available. We had a lawn with trees and rosebushes. Our house on Lindbergh Drive could have been found in any American neighborhood. A cinder block fence ringed the perimeter of base housing. Looking out, we could peer above the top of the fence and see a vast space, seemingly empty. But, when it rained in this part of the Mojave Desert, wildflowers appeared overnight; the blossoms lasting until the hot, dry winds and high temperatures returned.

So, our new life began. I do not think that we could have chosen a better place to begin a marriage or a career.

Let's deal with the professional side first. I was a Captain in the United States Air Force and a Flight Surgeon at Edwards Air Force Base, a test facility in the middle of the Mojave Desert. It was exciting to be at Edwards in the early '60s. John Glenn had orbited the earth 18 months earlier. Now, America was serious about winning the space race. Edwards' high-profile mission as a flight test center guaranteed the base was staffed with outstanding civilian and military test pilots, engineers, and scientists. As the U.S. was in a race with the Soviet Union for a lunar landing, funding for the research and testing efforts was readily available. This base was an important stop on any politician or foreign dignitary's tour of military installations. Both the Air Force Space School and the Flight Test School, which produced many future astronauts, were located there. During this time, the X-15, an experimental plane with rocket engines, was undergoing testing at Edwards. There was also a rocket propulsion lab and testing facility about 20 miles from the main base. Edwards Air Force Base was and still is part of the Air Force Systems Command (AFSC). AFSC probably had more officers and civilians with Ph.D.'s assigned to its bases than any other Air Force group. Some commands such as Strategic Air Command or ADCOM, the American Defense Command, have been blended into other groups or eliminated because the Air Force mission has changed since the '60s, but AFSC remains intact.

As Edwards was isolated, it seemed to us that like other outposts in far-flung regions, personnel either were miserable or happy with very little feelings in between. Even though she was only 23 years old and I was fast approaching 40, Charlotte, a social creature, happily joined every activity open to women. For my part, and as this is my memoir, I consider Edwards my best assignment.

My primary responsibility was in support of flying personnel; as a secondary job, I had to serve as MOD. That's Medical Officer of the Day, which means when I was the MOD, I handled all the medical calls overnight during the week and on the weekend from Friday at 1800 (5:00 pm) until 0800 (8:00 am) Monday morning.

The base hospital, the only medical facility within 50 miles, had about 40 beds. Physicians, including two general surgeons, one internist, a pediatrician and an obstetrician/gynecologist were assigned to the hospital. The hospital commander was also a physician, but he did not take call. All the other physicians were usually MOD one night each week and one weekend per month. When we were on call we acted as emergency room physicians and provided care for any inpatient problems. We also delivered babies! Believe me when I say I preferred taking care of flying personnel.

It was the first time in many years I had an opportunity to fly, and I'm not just talking about riding in the copilot's seat.

My office was near the flight line. I was like a child in a candy store. Every new plane, fighter and bomber was either being tested or flown as part of a wing or squadron. All the pilots knew I had pilot wings, since I wore them on my uniform. When it came time for the pilots to do proficiency flights (that is, to log additional flying time as part of their job) they often asked me to fly with them. This was part of my job. It was a momentous time in my career. I had started flying with the propeller-driven planes during the war and now I was riding in the latest, fastest, most complex and expensive aircraft in the world.

I did more than ride in these planes; I flew them! Occasionally, on these proficiency flights, and I want to emphasize these were not missions but flights flown for the express purpose of maintaining pilot-readiness, the plane's commander or pilot asked me to take the left-hand or pilot seat. Once airborne, I flew the plane. So, I had my own flying experience in the B-58 and the B-52. Let me tell you more about these planes. The B-58, also known as the Hustler, was a combination fighter-bomber. Basically, it had the speed of a fighter and the munitions-carrying ability of a bomber. This was also the plane in which I flew Mach 2, or twice the speed of sound. No, I was not the pilot on that flight. I was just happy to go along for the ride. In those days, it was still a fairly small club of those who had flown Mach 2.

The B-52 was the largest bomber in the U.S. inventory. One day, I was scheduled to ride along on a proficiency flight, but upon boarding, the pilot signaled that I should sit in the left-hand seat. There was a third passenger along that day, a visiting Canadian pilot. He was seated in the jump seat directly behind the pilot and me. That day we were to practice touch-and-goes or takeoffs and landings. I did about two or three of these maneuvers. Remember, this was the only eight-engine plane in the USAF arsenal. It was a long way from the four-engine propeller planes I had flown in 1945. After I'd completed a series of these takeoffs and landings, the official pilot turned to the Canadian officer and said, "Not bad for a flight surgeon." I am sure the Canadian did not realize that I was also a pilot. I've always wondered what he thought after hearing that statement.

There were many flying and testing missions at this base. The U-2 surveillance, or spy plane, designed for high altitude, was really built for a single occupant, but the squadron at Edwards had several planes with two seats. The U-2 outfit was identified officially as a Weather Reconnaissance Squadron. Even the physical location for the planes and operations was separate on the North Base. The squadron, which had its own flight surgeon, operated under the tightest security.

One day, I was offered a ride in a U-2. As the plane was not really designed to have two seats, the interior was cramped. The U-2 had exceptionally long wings. After landing and taxiing to a stop, ground personnel attached wheel supports on the ends of the wings so the sides would not tip and hit the ground. I sat in the back seat with a very limited viewing area. I leaned forward to see if I could see the wings being attached to the supports and I instinctively went to grab the stick in front of my seat; at the last moment, I looked down and saw that it was the handle for the ejection seat. After that, I contented myself with the limited view.

It was my job to observe and care for the pilots; flying with them was part of the process. Certainly, they had the right stuff to have been assigned to this base with its advanced missions, but pilots still had the usual problems associated with family and work. As a flight surgeon, I had to make sure they remained in good physical and mental health so they could fly safely.

Rocket engine testing played an important role in space flight development. The X-15 plane provided the most involved and advanced rocket testing at Edwards.

Joe Engle, who later became an astronaut for NASA, was an X-15 pilot in the early sixties.

In these test flights, the X-15 rocket plane was attached to the underside of a modified B-52. Joe stayed with the B-52 flight crew for the takeoff. Once the plane was airborne, he climbed down into the cockpit of the X-15 to take his place at the controls. After the experimental plane was released from under the mother ship, Joe started the rocket engines. The boost from the engines sent the X-15 high into the sky. Supersonic speeds and high altitude flying were normal during these flights.

Why was I involved? As a flight surgeon I was there to render assistance if Joe ran into a problem. Two locations were used in these missions: the flat, dry hard surface lakebeds at Edwards AFB and China Lake in southern Nevada. China Lake was about 150 miles from the takeoff point. On flight test days, I joined a helicopter crew along with an Air Force corpsman and we'd fly to the China Lake location. If there was a problem with the launch or flight of the X-15, the dry lakebed could provide an emergency runway.

Our Piasecki helicopter had two tandem rotors and was known as the "flying banana." On several trips, as we approached the flight line, the pilot would say, "Hey, you want to fly?" Of course, I'd say, "Sure". This was a new experience for me and although a helicopter requires different skills, it's still a flying machine. With the pilot sitting next to me, he could provide instructions on how to maneuver a completely different set of controls.

Both China Lake and Edwards Dry Lake were large and could provide the long runway these high-speed rocket planes needed. Later, during the time of NASA flights, the Edwards lakebed was used as the alternate landing site.

Many flight tests had a chase plane assigned to the mission. The F-104 served this role for the X-15 flights.

The chase plane pilot followed the X-15 on its path, making sure the engines had started and the rockets were doing their job of sending the X-15 skyward. When this was confirmed, the F-104 pilot flew back to where we were waiting, then skimmed low and fast above the dry lake. This was our signal we could pack up the emergency gear and return to Edwards.

Every new plane designed for Air Force use was flight-tested at Edwards. During our time, the C-141 and the B-70 were undergoing these tests. The C-141, a large cargo plane with jet engines, is still flying today.

One day, I received a call from its test pilot asking me to join him for a night flight. Again, as we walked to the aircraft, he told me to get in the left-hand seat. I did, happily, and got to do several touch-and-goes, this time at night and in a brand new plane not yet operational. These memories last a lifetime.

The B-70, built as a replacement for the B-52, had a tragic history. At the time, it was the fastest bomber, scheduled to go Mach 3, and the most expensive one to be built. We were at Edwards for its maiden flight. Unfortunately, two years later in 1966, it collided with a chase plane during a test flight. A third prototype had been built, but the project was canceled.

We were still living at Edwards AFB when President Lyndon Johnson let the cat out of the bag and unwittingly disclosed the existence of the SR-71, a high-speed reconnaissance plane. Known as the Blackbird, it was tested right under our noses. Large, black and made of titanium so it could escape the notice of radar, the SR-71 had an illustrious history until satellites made manned surveillance flight unnecessary.

These exciting flights and our interesting life were nothing compared to the next chapter. Our first child, Nicole Aurette, was born at the base hospital April 9, 1964. She was healthy and extraordinarily good-looking with blond fuzz on her head.

All my life experiences had not prepared me for this chapter. Diapers, sleep-deprived nights, worry about colds and the responsibility for another human being, this time my own daughter, carried a lot more apprehension than any flight testing or touch-and-go maneuvers.

More on Nicole later . . .

TDY or Temporary Duty is part of being in the Air Force. Everyone in the military experiences these short or long stays away from home. At this stage in my career, I had relatively few unaccompanied travel assignments. One trip, however, remains a highlight. Pilots from the Flight Test School were invited to tour European flight test school facilities in England, France, Germany, and Italy. As the flight surgeon, I accompanied 20 pilots for the two-week trip, September 1964. As usual, I wrote home. I'll let my letters describe portions of my trip.

18 September 1964

Mes Chéries,

The crossing in the C-118 was easy; we had stretchers in rows of three on top of each other, lined with sleeping bags. Half played cards, half slept. I played cards, (Ha, ha, ha!) Found Germany (Wiesbaden) much changed, more people, more houses, cars, and congregating prelates! (I saw many.) I had a large lunch at Evreux while waiting for the train, terrific! *Paté de canard,* salmon *en mayonnaise, entrecote grillé, patissière,* for four bucks, with service and wine (Côtes du Rhône). I miss you both tremendously, especially in the morning for breakfast (you know the usual ceremony with Nicole) "Nicole, Nicole, (Spit, Bubbles, Cooing) How much cream can the milk here produce!

With tender love and kisses, Gino

And, from my stay at the Cavalieri Hilton in Rome:

24 September 1964

Dearest Charlotte and Nicole,

Everything progressing very nicely. Left Wiesbaden Tuesday. Spent one day in Bitburg Air Base and arrived here Wednesday.

Today we were host to the Italian AF at a small test facility they have near the sea. The outstanding part of the day was the lunch-eon at an excellent restaurant near Castel Gondolfo, the summer Papal residence. Un-fortunately, Italian cooking doesn't quite pair up with the loveliness of the settings. This was an illustration of first magnitude. Except for the hors d'oeuvre, which were truly great (some of that red ham, thinly sliced on peeled *figues*) the rest was good: Gnocchi, mixed grill and vegetables, cream puffs for dessert. They served Moët cham-pagne for dessert, but only half a cup and I spilt mine! So, on the other hand, and you will see the pictures, a hillside location over-looking the flat plains of Rome to the north, surrounded by big fig trees, a terrace, swimming pool; A place to return to (I have the address). The Hilton, as you would ex-pect, is well appointed, comfortable, but ri-diculously expensive, poorly located. Prices, in fact, are an exploitation! Really, this is on-ly for rich widows, middle-aged, or more, businessmen and their secretary-mistresses. More on this later at home!. . . There will be more little dresses for the Chérie à son Pa-

pa, and perhaps a thing or two not listed here. Rome is the wonderful city it always is. Walking at night is the most gratifying experience for the mind. Well, I have been a very good boy as you knew I would, only one meal a day on the economy, no extra-spending for nothingness. I went to bed early tonight. For such an expensive room, might as well use it.... With all my love and devotion and kisses for you two. Gino

If I thought the room was expensive, which was reimbursed by the Air Force as we were on official travel, the cost for my laundry was even more shocking; so offensive to Charlotte that when she saw the bill on my return, she wrote to Conrad Hilton, asking him why one should pay more for laundry than for a room. Believe it or not, he replied, explaining that I was charged at a lower group rate than was normal for the room. He even signed the letter.

Our time at Edwards would soon end. So much had happened in three years. Charlotte and I had begun our married life; I had completed the first leg of my USAF career as a military officer and our darling daughter, Nicole, had been born. In the world around us, John F. Kennedy had been assassinated, Lyndon Johnson had assumed the presidency and the Gulf of Tonkin incident had taken place, an event that would soon transform all our lives.

PART II
LETTERMAN GENERAL HOSPITAL
1965-1968

We did not realize the significance of the last event I mentioned. In 1965, I was about to make another career move. At the age of 43, I was accepted as an internal medicine resident at Letterman General Hospital in San Francisco. This was a large Army training hospital at the Presidio, an incredibly beautiful forest preserve perched high above the Pacific Ocean, San Francisco Bay, and the Golden Gate Bridge. Letterman was built in the early 1900s and although it had been remodeled and updated, the original barracks-style wards were still in place.

Army post housing was scarce, so we bought our first house in Corte Madera, a suburb on the north side of the Golden Gate Bridge. Our home, which cost $30,000, was more than we could afford. But we were lucky; the Army was putting the finishing touches on a set of new town houses at the Presidio and nine months after we arrived, we were assigned lodging on the post. We rented our house and said goodbye to commuting across the Golden Gate Bridge twice daily. (I left for work before traffic started and departed long after it had ended, so a one-way trip was usually done in about 20 minutes. We were also issued tickets for the 25 cent fare to cross the bridge).

Any physician will tell you that being a resident is difficult and challenging, with long days and nights and little free time. Yet, it's part of the training. Certainly, the practice of medicine has changed dramatically since I was a resident, but some things never change. Patient care is still the most important part of a physician's role. Bedside and clinic care can make the difference in how a patient accepts and responds to the treatment.

Again, back to the hospital regimen. The interns, first, second and third-year residents were the students. The staff physicians were the teachers, assisted by the fellows, doctors who had completed their residency and now were doing advanced training in a subspecialty. This time I had climbed one rung of the ladder. We were carefully supervised but we had significant patient treatment responsibility.

Before I start on the day's routine, I want to go back to the hospital's layout. Each specialty had its own ward. These wards were in long, wooden, parallel rows, jutting outward with large windows along each side. Each side of the room was lined with beds. Curtains around each bed provided privacy. Bathrooms were at the end of the wards. VIP's were given the few private rooms attached to these wards.

When I grow up I want to be . . .

Every morning I met with the intern to discuss the patients' treatments for our ward. Most of the wards had 18-20 beds so we had our hands full. We'd order the tests, speak with the patient, talk to the relatives, and make endless phone calls to arrange and coordinate tests. The wards were so long I began a lifelong habit of resoling my black uniform shoes with thick rubber.

In addition to caring for the patients, we had daily rounds or patient visits with the chief of the service and the chief resident. On Saturday mornings, we had Grand Rounds. The entire medical staff met for two hours, seeing patients and discussing cases. After patient rounds, we gathered in a conference room for a talk by a guest lecturer, usually a physician from the University of San Francisco Medical School.

At Letterman, one Air Force officer was accepted in each specialty training program for that year. We stood out, not just because of the blue slacks under our white coats but also because of our attitudes. We tended to be less uptight than our Army counterparts. Although we never felt less than welcome, there was still a slight undercurrent of difference between the services.

That's why I was taken by surprise when I was asked to be the Chief Resident for my third year of training. Yes, this was an honor, but it was also a huge responsibility. Now, I was in charge. I organized Grand Rounds, selected the guest speakers, reported each morning to the Commanding Officer of Letterman, a Major General, and did all the usual work of a resident. I did not have to act as the Medical Officer of the Day, but in reality, I was the MOD for the entire department of medicine. The buck stopped at my desk. I also cared for the VIP patients. I was a busy fellow!

Meanwhile, back at our Washington Boulevard town home, Charlotte had discovered Julia Child. Mrs. Child was cooking her way through the first of her many PBS series. This may be the time to mention I had given Mrs. Child's first book, *Mastering the Art of French Cooking*, as my wedding gift to Charlotte. Charlotte always felt it was another sign of my romantic nature; remember the proposal?

Charlotte had learned to cook at home while growing up in rural Pennsylvania and had spent one year at Penn State University in the Department of Home Economics before transferring to nursing school. Her mother, an excellent cook, worked nights as a nurse so Charlotte was responsible for much of the meal preparation.

At Edwards, Charlotte started to use the recipes from Julia's book. She spent hours preparing special dinners. After Nicole arrived, the meals became less complex. However, when Charlotte started watching Julia's television programs, she realized good French cooking could be quickly prepared. Thanks to this new approach, we embarked along a pleasant culinary path with outstanding results, especially since San Francisco and California had wonderful produce and products available for the cook.

Through the years, Charlotte continued to buy and use every cookbook Julia published. The original book is dog-eared and splattered with food stains. In 2001, we had an opportunity to meet Julia Child in Santa Barbara. To prepare for the trip, Charlotte packed Julia's books in her suitcase and carried them all to California. Mrs. Child graciously signed all of them.

San Francisco was good to us, but because of our limited economic means and busy schedule, we had to find ways to enjoy the area without incurring extra expense. Our house on the Presidio was in the fog zone and every day during the summer months we had what looked like thick, white smoke rolling over our house. In the afternoon, the sky usually cleared. The city's temperature was cool; we never went without a jacket, even in summer. We could drive from our house overlooking the Golden Gate Bridge, down through the Presidio and its forest of tall eucalyptus trees, until we reached the halfway point between our street and the main post parade ground. There, we'd look in the distance and see the beautiful, sparkling San Francisco Bay, dotted with white sails and, sitting in the middle of the bay, Alcatraz island.

Our main entertainment revolved around food. So, it was with great excitement that we followed the newspaper's series on "Eating out in San Francisco for $2.00 or Less." I cannot tell you how many dinners we enjoyed at Ernie's Delicatessen, our favorite restaurant in this category for the three years we lived in San Francisco. The name was a mystery as it served delicious Chinese food. So what if we could see the crates of lettuce stacked on the floor outside the restrooms? It was cheap and tasty with local color provided at no additional cost.

Living in San Francisco meant we had many out-of-town friends. We were on everyone's scenic stop. Our pattern to entertain visitors was one we'd be happy to have today. The Coast Guard maintained an officer's club at the Observation Tower on Treasure Island, a small Navy outpost in the middle of the Bay, halfway across the Bay Bridge. The club was open for two hours before dinner. Drinks were served at the top level. There was no elevator, so we walked up five flights to reach the bar. From there, for the price of a cocktail, we had a 360-degree view of the San Francisco Bay and surrounding shore. We'd show our guests the view, watch the sunset and then proceed to one of the city's many restaurants for dinner. From there, we'd drive to Fort Mason, another Army post along the bay. From a strategic point of view, military installations generally have the best land. The bar in the officer's club jutted out over the Bay, and here we'd enjoy a nightcap before heading back to our home.

It was not a bad life, in spite of a hectic and difficult schedule.

I had been offered a position as a medical corps officer in Germany and we were excited to be going back to Europe. My parents were now living in Paris and I wanted them to meet Nicole.

However, life has a way of changing without warning. One morning in May 1968, just six months short of completing my residency, I received a call from the Air Force assignment officer for medical corps personnel. He told me he needed an internist for a Vietnamese military hospital in Saigon. This was a special assignment because the physician had to speak French and they wanted someone recently trained.

How many French-speaking internists, recently graduated, do you think there are in the United States Air Force? Well, I guess you could say the fellow I was replacing and me.

Now, I had to break the news to Charlotte. I knew she would not take it well. For once, I stopped my daily work and drove home to tell her directly. She was devastated. It was a one-year assignment with a single one-week R & R or rest and recreation leave, so life was going to be tough for all of us.

According to Charlotte, the worst part was the six months we had to think about it. If I could have started in one week, I think it would have been easier.

Charlotte has always been one to make lemonade from lemons, so after she discovered the Army would pay to transport her and Nicole, ship our furniture and a car and they could live in Hawaii for the year, she perked up. There could also be more opportunities to make it to Hawaii for a short break than if I had to fly to the continental U S.

FIFTEEN

....

A YEAR IN VIETNAM

You might not understand my surprise at being given orders to spend 12 months in Vietnam. Even though the bombing missions over North Vietnam made headlines for much of the war, it was very much an Army-and-Marine-led conflict. Operations conducted by the USAF did not require the large numbers of troops and support personnel necessary for battles waged on the ground. There was only one Air Force field hospital in South Vietnam. This facility at Cam Ranh Bay, built in a beautiful beach area along the northern coast of South Vietnam, was used for military members of any service whose injuries and health problems did not require intensive treatment or recovery time. If necessary, Cam Ranh Bay served as a first stop for seriously wounded military members before they were airlifted to the next staging area, Clark Air Base in the Philippines. After that, the most critically wounded were evacuated to Hawaii and/or eventually back to the mainland.

This may seem like a roundabout way of describing the Air Force medical mission in Vietnam in the late '60s, but it demonstrates relatively few medical corps officers would be needed, particularly if their training was not in a surgical or orthopedic specialty. None of my Army medical residency classmates were sent to Vietnam.

Our friend, Jack Saylor, the Air Force medical resident in the class that followed mine, insists I received orders because of Charlotte! I'm not sure this is true since it was well known I was French-born. In Charlotte's inimitable style, she encouraged me to take the foreign language proficiency exam so it would be clearly listed on my record. Charlotte, in her heart of hearts, thought this might result in a posting to the American Embassy in Paris.

With this change in assignment, we had to plan our lives for the next 12 months. I had been given a firm commitment to be reassigned to Ramstein Air Base, Germany, after my year in Vietnam. I was now a Major, and with that promotion I had achieved field grade status. I can't remember the additional perks beside more money in my paycheck, but more deference is accorded—along with the need to salute less.

The worst part was the waiting. I had to complete my residency and maintain my responsibilities as Chief Resident. In preparation for our three separate moves, the Army, which runs on paperwork and forms, kept us busy. Charlotte and Nicole were going to live on the economy in Honolulu, which meant we had to pack separate shipments—a small amount for our living needs in Hawaii, the majority of our furniture for storage and separate boxes for my move to Vietnam. The car required an entirely different set of forms. This was important because buying a car in Hawaii would have been cost prohibitive. For whatever reason, I insisted we sell my first new car, a Triumph TR-4, bought during our stay at Edwards. Charlotte always believed I just didn't want her driving a convertible around Oahu. I probably felt keeping it well maintained would be too expensive for us.

I replaced it with a 1960 Nash Rambler American! I do not have to say anything further.

Charlotte drove this car in Hawaii. It did not have power steering, automatic transmission, seat belts or air-conditioning so she took every opportunity to ride in her friend Gaye Chronister's Thunderbird, a car with a powerful cooling system.

In addition to moving 3,000 miles, we had to find a place for Charlotte and Nicole to live. That was relatively easy. We signed a lease to move into the Queen Emma

Gardens, a high-rise apartment tower still operating today.

There was no opportunity to go to France to see my parents, so I wrote and suggested they meet us in Lancaster. You have to remember flying was not an everyday occasion for them. My father had flown only a few times in his life. Unbelievably, they agreed and made what was surely an arduous trip. We met them at the airport in New York City and drove them to the Pennsylvania home of my mother-in-law, Madalyn Meekins, 160 miles away.

In spite of the culture shock, they enjoyed the trip. Part of their anxiety was relieved because Lancaster County has produce and foodstuffs that are equal to anything available in France.

We toured Washington and Philadelphia and even took my parents deep into Lancaster County so they could meet some of Madalyn's Amish friends. Aurette and Georges were more of a curiosity to the Amish than the Amish were to them. Maybe it was half and half. Even thinking about it 45 years later, I marvel that Aurette and Georges were willing to make a trip and that we could keep them safe and sound in such an unfamiliar environment.

My departure hovered above all our thoughts and conversations. I don't know how military men and women and their families who have returned repeatedly to

Iraq and Afghanistan do it. This is such a difficult separation. The pain is shared equally between the one who boards the plane or ship and the spouses and children who remain at home.

I was lucky; I knew my life would not be in peril, but I still faced the usual difficulties one confronts in a remote assignment, particularly in a combat area.

The night I left Hickam Air Force Base in Honolulu finally arrived. I think Charlotte and I had the same thought: Once the plane departed we could start counting the days until my return.

Much of what I have to say from here is contained in the letters I wrote to Charlotte and Nicole during our time apart.

It seems I started writing before I even arrived. In flight between Clark and Saigon:

> 1 October 1968
>
> My Darlings,
>
> Well, 2 hours away! From Hickam, where we were delayed because of a family not reporting on time, to Guam, 7 hours, long night! Breakfast, did not eat, too tired and dejected. Guam at 8 a.m., local 4 Oct. Pleasant surroundings. Guam, to Clark, 3 hr, good lunch on board, felt better, ate it all, slept. Clark at 10 local—Now 2 hr. 15 min. to V-N. Departed 12:20, should arrive by 3 pm—so

not bad. I kept the time from Honolulu so I have followed your day. Now 7 pm, maybe you went to the beach. I am quite anxious to see what is in store over there beyond the horizon. The weather has been superb all along, hot, yes, but not exaggeratedly and all those terminals are cool. You should see the traffic! People everywhere, going, coming. This Pacific Ocean is crossed in two steps like jumping a stream. They are going to serve a snack now and I have my pill all ready to be swallowed. [Everyone serving in Vietnam had to take anti-malaria pills . . . as another bit of personal history; I had had malaria as a child.]

Nicole, again, you will have to be a big girl and help Mommy with the house and yourself until I come back. When you go to school and learn more letters and figures send them to me. Mommy will take you to the beach often I am sure, behave well! I stayed all day in the big airplane, a green one. Lots of love and kisses, Take care. All is and will be well. Gino

I didn't wait long to send the next letter. One day later . . .

4 October, 8 pm

Dearest Darlings,

Well, since it is free, might as well use it and write. (Letters from Vietnam did not require postage.) Around 15:00; have gone through the never-ending procedure of clearing in. In essence, I am under MACV (Medical Army Command Vietnam.) But nothing yet as to work. An E-3 (enlisted rank pretty near the bottom of the ladder) did the initial briefing and did not know much. Tomorrow more briefing, I shall learn more. Tonight, I am temporarily bedded at MACV, Ton Son Nhut and new barrack type with 24 beds on one floor, no partition; Mind you, the company grade (lieutenants and captains) has double bunks! The initial impression is drab, very drab. The people are nice enough, smile, mobile faces. The air traffic is constant. Helicopters and transports. Ate in the mess hall tonight and got my first taste of things to come. 7am. 5 Oct. First night . . . did not sleep too well. I'm still on Hawaii Time. Constant sound of distant explosions, probably cannon. Will mail this one after breakfast—more news this afternoon. By by, Baisés, Gino

Note, please, that once again I was sleeping in a room with 24 beds! But not for long:

5 October 1968

My Darlings,

Long day, during which I tried to accomplish a lot but I am not sure that I did. Let's start from beginning. First, missed breakfast, since it closes at 7:30 instead of 8:00 as we were told. However, had coffee and cake (free) then attempted to go to Main Base.

Now this Ton Son Nhut is an inextricable mix-up of civilian and military [both nations] complexes; traffic in between is horrible. The Vietnamese have bicycles and the motorbikes with young GI drivers by the hundreds run all around them. I found a military bus, which after many detours took me where I wanted to go.

My first attempt to locate mail was unsuccessful. There are three different post offices. I went to the two wrong ones before being told about the right one, although it is not proven right since I have not gone yet (too late) and therefore don't know. Then BX. Disappointed! Prices every bit the same as stateside except again liquor (who cares!) Champagne, one brand Mumm Cordon

When I grow up I want to be …

Rouge, $3.50 Not bad, but not given away either.

Then return to MACV compound, lunch, cafeteria, (horrible!) I shall stick to mess hall until I get my permanent billet. There are more briefings this afternoon. I am under MACV, will be in Saigon but yet, where or what type of work, not known yet. I have to report to MACV Surgeon office to know. Will do that tomorrow.

OK, to dinner, I have met a Master Sergeant from my time in Germany. We go to dinner together. *Milles baisérs et tendresses.* Gino

Two days later, I wrote:

7 October 1968

Mes Chéries

At last, they woke up at MACV Surg. And somebody came down and asked for me, 1st Lt. male nurse, U.S. Navy who is going to work with me at Cong Hoa. He had all the info. Here they are—I am going to be the only U.S. physician around with him and corpsman driver. We have a Jeep. We live in a BOQ situated not too far from where I am now. Two to a room, private bath, one refrigerator for 9 rooms!!! Maid

171

service, complete with wash, shoeshine. I will be moving probably tomorrow. We work Vietnamese hours, which are very conservative 8-11 and 2-4 give or take a ½ hour. The rest of the time, do as you please. I am going to try and talk the colonel into using me in aviation medicine.

As I reread these letters, I marvel at my single-mindedness. I was determined to return to flying status! As background; I received several hundred dollars extra each month as a medical corps officer. I also received hazardous duty pay for serving in a combat region and if I had a slot as a flight surgeon I would receive flight pay as well. Not only did I want to fly, I also looked forward to the extra money.

But, I wasn't sent to Vietnam as a flight surgeon. Remember, I was there because I spoke French! It was up to me to secure a posting as flight medical officer with a flying outfit. During my first couple of months in Vietnam, I mentioned speaking to someone in one office or another, asking how I could get on flying status. Eventually that happened and I spent many non-hospital duty hours flying all around the Orient, not to mention three trips to Hawaii!

Back to my main job as an advisor/teacher to the military hospital at Cong Hoa . . . I had lots to say in my letters to Honolulu.

I am now installed in my job at Cong Hoa; there are good days when I feel I am doing something and bad days when I feel could just as well stayed home. At the bottom is my realization that they could have used in-country doctors to do that, simply rotating one, Army or USAF, every month or so. My schedule is now well fixed. 0745, Jeep to MACV, 0810, Jeep to Cong Hoa, 0830, Rounds in a ward, alternate each day of week, with one of the six trainees. 11:30 Jeep to Mess, Lunch, rest . . . 1345 Jeep to MACV-1410 to Cong Hoa, 1430-1630. Varied conferences in which I participate. 1630 Jeep back to BOQ. By 1900 I am in the room for the night. Flying a little is going to enliven this routine.

The details around me, of the first few days do not strike me any more. The traffic, the heat, the dirt, the hospital itself with its despondent pitiable look, make only a fleeting impression in a state where I am rather perfunctorily moving.

The work was frustrating and not particularly rewarding.

22 November

Tonight I operated (retractors—I held the skin and organs apart so the surgeon could see his work area) with Garza until 19:30 because he can't find V.N. doctors to do it. Garza is really a surgeon's surgeon. He love to cut, does 3 majors a day and by golly if those V-N don't learn from him, they will never learn. They will never learn! Would you believe, Garza and I operating at 7:30 pm alone in the whole damn surgical service with 3 OR's, not a single V-N doctor. The last one quit in the middle of the procedure because he had to catch his transportation to go home. And still 8 or 10 wounded VN soldiers brought in from the interior waiting in the receiving room. Garza showed me a face burn and said this one has been here 4 hours, nobody even washed his face! That is the Vietnamese physician sense of responsibility toward the their countrymen. In surgery they are absolutely ignorant! They must have a 50% mortality surgical rate due to inept management. They survive on pride. The patients don't! On the medical service, this is not too notable! Mistakes, yes, but

not so blatant, with such catastrophic results.

My feelings about the work continued in another letter.

13 December

The work seems to have slowed down
somewhat after initial period of enthusiasm,
same with Garza. We'll have to find ways of
rebuilding momentum. My boys are learning a few things— some good things. Tomorrow, giving them small examination,
questions extracted from medical assessment exam. Will be fun. On the surgical side
it is a great pity. They just fail miserably in
taking care of those poor wounded. They
have an unnecessary mortality of 50% due to
poor to non-existent fluid management,
wound sepsis, disorganization, lack of interest. They were never taught. They never
sought learning! There is no OJT in surgery!
Medicine is slightly different. Their pathology is 90% infectious so anybody can give
antibiotics. Although they manage not to
give enough, or too late, and if only they
stopped giving steroids to everybody! One
of my boys feels poorly— OK, so what!
Prednisone! Why, Why? So, now he has

some loss of T-waves on EKG, and one cannot tell if it is the steroids or a pericarditis
or else. I think we are spoiled; we have everything in medicine and more. They have
nothing and even that nothing they manage
to spoil. No cardiac catheterization, no cardiac surgery, lots of valvular disease from
rheumatic fever, lots of congenital defects,
all things that we promptly dispose of in
U.S.A! Here they just go on their disappearing way.

My roommate, Luis, a brilliant Army surgeon from
Puerto Rico, was a good companion for this year away
from home. We were lucky because we had our own
Jeep, which gave us the freedom to go anywhere at any
time. Luis drove at first, but after a couple of attempts to
maneuver through the crowds, he gave up and I took
over the responsibility of getting us from Point A to
Point B. Not easily accomplished, as I noted in a letter to
Charlotte.

There is a large high school on the way
to MACV from here. I have driven by at
school-out time: a large flow of white flowing robes for the girls, white shirts, black
shorts for the boys. They slowly roll back
traffic on the road, forming a large plug of
white. It is mayhem; 10-ton trucks, smoking,

belching black diesel makes threading a passage among them with blaring horns. A little
boy faces huge wheels with millimeters to
spare—a miracle. Thousands of motorbikes
now flow, zigzag through; with the Jeep at
every yard of the road, we almost hit someone or something. The salvation is that we
go so slow in this sea that there is no danger to persons. We just push. It is not uncommon to see four people on a motorbike,
two adults, 2 or 3 children. Front, back, in
between. And, they all wave, smile, dart
through left, right of the Jeep, both direc-
tions at once. Someone, male or female,
waits unconcerned at the roadside. Small
nude infants play in the dirt feet away from
the stream, unbroken stream of trailer trucks
driven by shirtless, sweaty, tanned, unconcerned young Americans. All this bathed in
a whitish exhaust smoke from the 2-cycle
motorbikes, which burn oil in gas.

You may have noticed by now much of this memoir
deals with flying and food. In my next sentence, I revert:

Did I tell you that they make regular
French bread on the economy? White,
crusty as can be. But offered on open stands,
among the dust, the smoke, handled by

those hands! However, in town, there are regular bakeshops, with protected display and they pack the bread in plastic bags. The maid brought me one the day before. She guaranteed the cleanliness! So I ate it. Real good, a little spongy from the plastic bag and the heat, but tasty of sweet French bread. Will have more.

But that was not the only thought I had on my mind. I was already planning for Nicole's future as a musician:

Saigon

29 January

Nicole,

I shall hang up your pretty drawings and coloring, the alarm clock and the bowling pin. When will you start music lessons? Mommy, look into that. I think if they are available, she should begin!" Nicole was four at the time I wrote this.

My year in Vietnam was probably unique in that I faced little physical danger apart from driving in the traffic. In relating my experiences, I do not want to diminish in any way the hardship and horrors of war that were seared in the minds of Americans. Those of us who served in Vietnam have our own experiences and most likely our view of the war years are based on the time we spent in country. I note in rereading these letters my own ambivalence about my life there and my feelings about the conflict. There was much to admire about the Vietnamese, but they had been fighting since the early '50s, first to end French rule, and later with the attempt to resist the advances of the Communists who controlled the northern part of the country.

In January I wrote about my trip to Can-Tho:

> . . . which is the largest town in the Delta and visited the military V-N hospital there; I am the representative of professional services on this committee that travels to several hospitals to establish construction and improvement needs for 1971. We are planning ahead. I was much surprised to find a very clean place, very well run, flower beds, clean wards, hard-working people. Very reassuring. I told them so. I think that it emerges that Cong Hoa is a political place, totally non-devoted to patient care but devoted to harboring a preferred crowd near Saigon, so that, in turn, that crowd can happily go after its own private interests. It is a poor, poor, place for patients, advantageous for physicians.
>
> We flew bright and early, arrived at 07 AM or so, and waited one hour for transportation Needless to say, we landed at the mil-

itary airfield and Jeeps were sent to the civilian airfield! It is guaranteed that had we landed at the civilian airfield, Jeeps would have dutifully gone to the military airfield. The Mekong River or one of its branches flows along the town. The Navy is all over with landing crafts, river patrol boats, etc. It even has its own helicopters and uses the whole thing as poetically named, Riverine Force When we fly MACV missions like that, we get special HQ transportation, usually V-21 Army, trim turboprop, quite fast and good service. We had the airplane to ourselves, like executives—3 Vietnamese, 4 U.S. officers. Took us down, brought us back. No wait, no registration. It is all arranged the night before. Why do you think the war costs so much? My French is of tremendous advantage in these groups. They always end up clustering around me, whether I translate or promote conversation. The rest of the committee would like my presence all the time, but of course, I can't and Garza is also a designated member and gets half the trips. I'll probably go to Danang Monday. Well, it's all part of the game! Although this is serious. There are decisions involved and money, too, lots of it. There will be lots of other committees and committee members before these decisions are all made. The big fear that the V-N has now is that we clear the place without delay. They cannot dream of directing their own affairs without support. After the French, us. They find it hard to take, after us, they themselves.

I am going through a period of complete resignation; I need something to get me out of it. I am afraid only seeing you and the little one would shake me out of this melancholy. Love, big as mountains and kisses numerous as falciparum mosquitoes in Vietnam. Gino

The number of letters I wrote not only to Charlotte and Nicole, but to my parents and brothers and even Mme Moquereau, the woman with the chestnut jam at the Maison Belge, provided a lengthy account of my days and nights in Vietnam. I look at them today and I wonder how work is done without computers or cell phones.

Orders rule your life in the military. I'm sure orders still get lost even with the miracle of electronics. You can't do anything without them. You have orders to move, either temporarily or permanently, to new assignments, so my orders to Vietnam were to assist the South Vietnamese medical efforts at a Saigon military hospital. Sprinkled throughout these pages is my interest in flying. Since I was not in a primary flying slot as a flight surgeon, I had to apply for a spot to receive orders. Usually, once you have a medical specialty as I did, being on flying status takes a secondary role. However, I was determined and within three months of arrival in Vietnam, I secured a slot.

Now, I had an opportunity to fly! The time spent away from my family passed more quickly. I worked at Cong Hoa during the day and after dinner I went to the flight line at the military airport in Saigon and looked for a flight that would return by morning.

Saigon

26 March

I now have 32 missions. The last time I flew, Saturday night, I went to Dong Hoa, which is on the DMZ (demilitarized zone) about 3-4 miles south. It was just like landing anywhere else, GCA, landing radar, positive control radar all the way in, runway lights, the works, we are right at the DMZ. The DMZ was close to the border with North Vietnam so one expected enemy activity. No problems. We stayed there 45 minutes, unloading, loading until midnight.

Not a peep! A few flares, distant cannon fire,
like Saigon. On the return trip, stopping in
Danang, I listened to a young captain who is
traffic officer at airlift control. He said,
"What you read in the paper and what you
experience here is different!" In other
words, even Danang is quiet, probably the
same as Saigon. My information is mount-
ing that we are bombing the hell out them!
Laos right along the border with NVN. Really over 500 sorties a day, including B-52's.
Now I can see why—in spite of an alleged
30,000 troops a month and corresponding
materiel crossing, they can't show more of
an effort that I feel nothing anywhere I go. I
am prepared to wager that they lose 50% of
all that goes down the trail. Do you know,
and I keep track, that practically since I have
been here, the enemy has never engaged,
never, more than a battalion size force! And,
do you know that somewhere south of here,
the NVA has recently engaged a company
made entirely of girls. Good sign, very good
sign. I have a copy of a USARVN Medical
Bulletin and it contains a review of the Med
Evac system of the enemy. It points out it
takes from 2-7 days or more for them to get

wounded to a place where definitive surgical care is available. 7 days of walking!! Carrying the wounded on a hammock strung on a pole. I told you at least 50% of the wounded died.

I harbored a secret desire to see some evidence of conflict. As I described the traffic on the streets in Saigon, it was apparent I was more likely to face danger while driving than on one of my flights. However, one day I was on a routine mission aboard a C-130. I was seated in the jump seat between the pilot and copilot. We were in the landing pattern on the downwind or left side of the runway when suddenly I spotted several explosions hitting the runway. I mentioned this to the pilot, who called the tower. He was told a South Vietnamese pilot had mistakenly dropped his bombs on takeoff. Fortunately, there was an alternate runway for us to land.

And, so the time passed. I made two extra trips to Hawaii as part of the medical team aboard air evac planes. These flights carried wounded personnel to Tripler Army Hospital on Oahu for care that couldn't be handled in Vietnam or the Philippines. Having two breaks like this in addition to the normal seven-day R & R leave divided the year into manageable segments. By July, we were beginning to count the days.

We were busy in Saigon. As the headquarters for military medical affairs, we routinely handled health issues involving government officials from both countries.

Saigon

3 July

One day the Prime Minister of Vietnam was admitted to the U.S. hospital for cataract surgery. I am taking care of him medically. It is going to be touchy because he has to stay at bed rest and for a 67-year old man, that means atalectesis (lung collapse) cramps, phlebitis and what not.

But all was well.

8 July

My Darling,

Ouf! Today at 7 pm, the Prime Minister was discharged from the hospital. No doubt that he was most happy, full of praise and thanks for "not only the care, but the feelings behind the care," he said in French, bien sûr and I, playing no small role, in my unassuming manner, translating, adding, in mellifluously [Note from Charlotte: Gino sometimes makes up words.] tones; I would be an excellent ambassador or general! No doubt! Every morning during his stay, I had to brief General Neel, who would brief General Abrams who probably in turn would call Ambassador Bunker. And Gino at the beginning of this chain .... Already, the PM has invited us three, the ophthalmologist, surgeon and myself to dinner at his house.

Later in the same letter, I wrote:

... to complete my international activities; I had lunch with the Thai Surgeon as his guest in a Chinese restaurant in Saigon. You have to surmount the initial recoil at the street in front, the dirt, and the smell. Then the staircase with the broken mirrors, the janitor eating his rice, sitting on a stool, while picking his feet and you then imagine what the kitchen looks like. Alas, you have to go through it. Too late to turn around and flee. Surprise! The dining room is gay, well decorated, the table is pleasantly set, china, fluffed up napkins, and clean tablecloth. Allons [Let's go] it is not so bad after all. Chinese menu, crowned by a whole big broiled fish served with mushrooms, vegetables, delicious! But a sweet river type fish. Leechees for dessert. The Thai had brought a bottle of their own Thai made liquor, a cross between brandy-whiskey and what not. Very tasty, little sweet, not too strong. Enjoyed it.

July 1969 was a momentous month with the first moon landing. Like everyone else, we were captivated.

Saigon

23 July 1969

It is really a needed boost, that lunar landing. We can land a little contraption upside down on the moon. Gee whiz! Everybody loves us for a few days. All the world. You know, on the morning of the moon landing, I turned the radio on at 1 am and I heard the first sentence "They are now face down." I don't know why, but I immediately thought they had landed face down. I was crushed. I froze for two minutes; I could not hear a word more. Then I realized they were flying face down. To see better! Whoofff!!

Darling, letter writing is an uneven business. Well, all this is irrelevant! I LOVE YOU. YOU LOVE ME. Gino

My letters reflect my short timer status. I was scheduled for my third trip to Honolulu and after my return from that short stay, there would only be six weeks until I left for good.

Saigon

22 July (18 days)

My Darling,

In the midst of great joy due to the success of our moon landing I come to tell you that last night I attempted to write to you, but was unsuccessful in that I fell asleep on the paper. This week has been so different as I already depicted to you. Additionally, I had dinner at the Prime Minister's house Sunday night. Therefore the night was sleepless as usual after a large meal *arrosée de vin et d'alcohol* [sprinkled with wine and alcohol.] Suffice it to say that it was absolutely terrific, demonstrating that any cooking, in this case Vietnamese, done with talent can be superb. The P.M. gave me his signed photo. Being sleepless allowed me to hear the moon landing, which occurred at 4 am here.

Hawaii, especially Honolulu, was an expensive place to live. Even in 1968, most parents worked outside the home, so nursery schools were on a six-hour schedule and kindergarten didn't end until after 3 p.m. That reduced the time parents had to worry about childcare. Nicole, who arrived in Oahu having already been to nursery school, entered the Nuuanu Baptist School for a pre-kindergarten term. She did so well she was selected to go to a summer pilot program at the University of Hawaii for gifted students. Was ever a father so proud?

Saigon

28 June 1969

My darling little Nicole,

Mommy tells me that you are now going to a new school at the university. Surely it is a quick progress for a 5-year-old girl. From nursery school to university. I am very proud of my daughter. I want you to tell me what you are learning, the new songs or new stories. Also congratulations for swimming to the raft. Did you do it by yourself? I am proud of you for that too! You know that I shall come in August to Honolulu for five days again. After, I shall come back in October for good, for good! I shall bring presents and chocolate candy and champagne for you in August. I love you very, very much and I send you many kisses. Be a good girl. Your Daddy Gino

No goofing around for our little princess. If you remember, I had already mentioned piano lessons to her but I wasn't done yet:

Saigon

2 August

My darling daughter, I will be coming home soon with presents. I think of you a lot and everything mommy tells me about you is a cause for great pleasure. When we go to Germany you will learn to ski and mommy too. Because now she knows she can. I was in Singapore and got you a nice surprise there. I am impatient to see your new dress and new hairdo. In one week we shall all go to the beach together. *Bonjour, bonsoir au Clair de la Lune Mon Amie* Nicole. Love, Daddy

Finally, the end was in sight.

30 September 1969 (3 days)

Darling, this will be the last letter. It is something. HURRAH! Sign out begins today. Went to Bangkok yesterday and Formosa on Sunday. All is fine. See you very, very soon. Gino

I look back on my year in Vietnam and I have mixed feelings. Certainly, the separation from Charlotte and Nicole was difficult, but apart from the long absences I had an opportunity to see them three times during that year, a situation not available to most. I also managed to fly as much as was possible given that I had a day job.

Life in this country was a study in sharp contrasts. So much good and so much less so . . . the dirt, the squalor, the disease, and for the South Vietnamese, eventually, the takeover by the Communists meant continued hardship. What were we doing there? What was our mission? There were so many deaths and injuries. The survivors and their families have not forgotten. Those of us who participated remember being in the first conflict in which the U.S. did not emerge the victor. For me there will always be regret that our time in Vietnam did not bring the changes we hoped for. I know what they could have achieved without the Communist takeover.

I do not keep up with the story of life in Vietnam today, but I know the desire for freedom always exists. Look at the number of Vietnamese who have immigrated to the U.S. I believe they are the most entrepreneurial group in our society today. Their successes are everywhere. From music to medicine, nail salons to restaurants and commercial fishing, the Vietnamese work hard and become productive and valuable members of our country.

....

SIXTEEN

GERMANY,
THE SECOND TIME AROUND

O ctober is a month of remembrances for Charlotte and me . . . some good, some not so good and some that are really, really important. Charlotte's birthday is on the 10th of the month. We're all happier if I don't forget it!

But, for this memoir, October signifies beginnings and endings. I left for Vietnam in October 1968, I returned from there, October 3, 1969, and our plane touched down in Germany, October 30. What a contrast from my arrival in Vietnam one year earlier. Instead of heat, humidity and the crush of people, we found fall temperatures, nearly constant rain, and organization.

In the service, when you have a change of station, or a new assignment, you have a sponsor. This is usually someone with whom you will work. A good sponsor shows you around and helps ease the settling in process. At an overseas assignment, the unfamiliarity of the country adds to the importance of a good sponsor. We were lucky; we had Lowell Suckow, a pediatrician, and his wife Margaret Ann as our sponsors. We are fortunate to count the Suckows as our friends today, 40 years after he drove from Ramstein Air Force Base to Rhein Main Air Base to meet us.

I remembered the last time I arrived in Germany. I was an Airman First Class then and now I was a Major in the Medical Corps! I'm not sure whether to consider this leap in rank and status as speedy or not. In the past 13 years, I had completed medical school, internship and residency, married, had a daughter and spent a year in Vietnam. I had been busy. Now, I was ready to enjoy my return to Europe.

I can report that our departure from Hawaii was uneventful. We had sent the Nash Rambler ahead, a necessary step since we wanted to have a car when we arrived in San Francisco, our point of entry. It was there, awaiting our arrival. After visiting friends and family, including Charlotte's brother, David Smith, we began our drive east, ending in New Jersey, where we shipped the car to Germany.

I won't go into excruciating detail about our 3,000-mile journey across the United States with our five year old daughter Nicole. This was pre-videos, Game Boys, and even Etch-a-Sketch. Instead, there were miles and miles of I Spy, singing and many stops.

It was during one of those stops that we had our sole misstep. Charlotte loves to tell this story because she thinks it's representative of the way I think and act. Somewhat compulsively, according to her. However, no one I know wants Charlotte, with her free spirit, to fly a plane. We had stopped for gas on the Will Rogers Turnpike between Oklahoma City and Tulsa late on a Sunday afternoon. I kept track of the keys. It was safer that way.

I think during our married life the words I have heard Charlotte say most often are "Where's my ___?" Fill in the blank. Keys, purse, ring, watch, you name it. Charlotte is too busy to bother with little things. I prefer order, knowing that if I always place them in the same spot, I will know where to find them. I cannot walk barefoot in the house or anywhere else, other than the beach. My slippers have to be perfectly lined up at the side of the bed where I can slip into them. I'm not sure I could get up if they weren't there. As an added reason for this care, I believe that if you walk barefoot in Charlotte's house, you deserve what you step in. It's not only Charlotte; the cats offer a daily road map of where they've been, what they've eaten and even evidence of their most basic functions.

I did not trust Charlotte to carry the extra set of keys. They were locked in my briefcase safely stowed in the trunk. I got out of the car, opened the trunk door, laid my keys inside so I could retrieve something and then without thinking, shut the lid. Suddenly we had no keys and no hope of getting any. In those days, you could not find a locksmith who would drive 40 miles on a Sunday afternoon. We tried everything, but nothing worked, and eventually we had to pry the lid open. For the duration of our trip, our trunk was held shut with a piece of rope tied around the bumper.

After spending several days with Madalyn, we drove to McGuire Air Force Base to board the plane to our new home. In those days, the Air Force operated a Military Air Command (MAC) service. Dependents were authorized to fly on military-sanctioned flights (in this case, a charter from one of the airlines) as long as the origin or arrival was outside the continental United States. The car went by ship to the German port of Bremerhaven.

We were welcomed with a certain amount of fanfare. I was slated to become the Chief of Professional Services for the USAF Dispensary at Ramstein. In the Air Force the hierarchy was as follows: The commander was a physician or Medical Corps officer. The second in command, the Chief of Professional Services or Medical Services, (if the clinic does not have inpatients) was also a physician. The administrator, an MSC officer (Medical Service Corps), was not a physician.

I had been disputing my date of rank with the USAF Office of Personnel for years. All decisions regarding pay and promotion depend on the initial date of service. To further complicate this regulation, physicians are credited for rank and pay based on date of graduation from medical school. As I mentioned, the French medical school system awards M.D. status after the internship. Technically, I was not a physician until I had completed my internship in Buffalo, the sixth year of my medical school training. This status is granted upon graduation from medical school in the U.S., so I believed my date of service was one year earlier than was listed on my official record. Two months after our arrival at Ramstein Air Base, the change to my record was suddenly approved. This meant I had completed the necessary time in grade for major. Within days, I was promoted to Lt. Colonel!!! Not bad when you think my last promotion on German soil had been to Staff Sergeant.

Charlotte still remembers the date she and the hospital commander pinned on my silver oak leaves—January 20, 1969. This was a nice start to our tour in Europe. Now, we had to have a suitable mode of transportation, something other than the Nash Rambler.

Part of our mission during the year we were separated was to save $5,000, the purchase price for a new Mercedes. Mission accomplished. We arrived in Germany with adequate funds to order a new 280 SE sedan. In those days, there was always a plan. We could take advantage of a Canadian buying system to avoid the 11% tax that would be due if we bought it with our U.S. papers. The Canadians, through their PX, purchased the car, took a small handling charge and then sold it to us. It was all about the paperwork. No one drove the car until we showed up on January 27, 1970, at the factory in Sindelfingen, a town near Stuttgart. We had a tour of the factory, then lunch in their restaurant—white tablecloths and all. Finally, the big moment arrived. We were escorted to a special section where our beautiful car was waiting. A Mercedes representative went through the essentials; we signed more papers and we were ready to go. A couple from the air base drove with us to Sindelfingen so we could both ride back to Ramstein in the Mercedes.

What an experience! We took extra care and drove home at a sedate speed. That would change later as we entered into the German sport of trying to outrun as many cars on the Autobahn as possible. My top speed was 120 miles per hour, although I really went that fast only one time. Normally, I kept it between 100-110. Again, that's mph, not kilometers. Can you imagine? This was 1970.

There are two things you learn when you drive on the Autobahn: never attempt to pass on the right side of another car and stay in the right lane unless you are ready to pass. If you're driving a fast car—and our 280SE qualified—you will have to share the left lane with few cars other than Porsches and BMW's. Those days of fast driving are gone, but we enjoyed them while we were there. Do you realize we still have the "Green Mercedes?" The odometer has turned over three times so we have driven more than 300,000 miles. We had it restored about 10 years ago, but we don't drive it often as changing gears is a finicky task. I am sure if we were to take it on the highway and "open it up" it would still go like the wind. My mother used to say that riding in it was like taxiing down an airplane runway.

As the Chief of Professional Services, I monitored the professional activities of the physicians on the staff and, treated patients in the medical clinic. Besides these duties, I had a flying slot, so again I had a chance to get some time in the air. That part of the mission I did not consider work. I was busy and there were many challenges, but after a long, arduous residency and the rigors of Vietnam, the problems in Germany seemed easy to handle.

My greatest work challenge was Colonel X, the hospital commander. That wasn't his name, but in this case, I think it's better if I don't use it. He had a difficult, mercurial personality and was feared and disliked by the staff members.

I didn't have a choice; I worked for him directly and our offices were in the command section separated by the secretary's desk.

I doubt that Colonel X would have risen to the rank of colonel if he had been anything but a physician. During the Vietnam War era, medical corps officers were in short supply. In the pre-volunteer force days, most physicians lamented and often resented the time they had to spend as military physicians, this in spite of the fact our pay was higher than any line officer in our grade. Relatively few physicians chose the less lucrative path of serving in the armed forces. Today, with the precarious state of health care and the regulations facing those in medical practice, I suspect the relatively stress-free career as a military physician probably has more appeal.

I can remember two episodes that demonstrated Colonel X's behavior. One afternoon, I was in my office speaking long distance with someone in a Swiss hospital. We were discussing the transfer of a Ramstein airman who had been injured in a skiing accident. I assume I was talking in a loud voice. (Charlotte believed all Europeans of my generation thought when you made long distance calls you had to talk louder to be heard.) The secretary poked her head in the door, raised her finger to her lips and said, *Shhh* very gently. I couldn't understand why she was telling me to speak more softly. Rank has its privileges. After I had completed the call, I went to ask her why she had come into my office when I was on the phone. She apologized profusely, but said she had orders from Colonel X that he couldn't be disturbed during his afternoon nap and she was afraid I might wake him.

My favorite Colonel X memory is true. At the bank on base, O-6 officers, full colonels, were given the privilege of meeting with the branch manager who would handle their requests rather than have them stand in line like the rest of us. Colonel X went to the bank one day, walked into the manager's empty office and sat down. He waited a few minutes and when the manager didn't appear, he looked around and spotted a buzzer mounted on the wall. Assuming he could call for assistance, he pushed the button. All hell broke loose. The iron gates at the bank entrance slammed shut, the sirens started wailing and within a minute or two, armed police showed up with their guns drawn. This episode became base lore. Typically, Colonel X thought all he had to do was press a button and he'd receive the attention he deserved. He certainly did this time, but I don't think it was what he expected.

Colonel X knew that he had a problem dealing with others. One day he confessed to me that the dispensary would run much more smoothly if he stayed in his office and let me handle the problems and the personnel. I had learned to handle him by taking his quirks in stride and treating him with respect. Underneath the bluster, Colonel X was a kind man. I was sorry to say goodbye when I drove him to the airport for his return to the states.

My French language skills led to another enjoyable episode in my professional life. In 1972, I was asked to write a paper and present it in English and French at a conference in Libourne, France. This small town in Bordeaux, just minutes away from St. Emilion and Château d'Yquem vineyards, was the site of the "Sixth Conference of Advanced Training for Young Military Physicians." For me, the word *young* was not particularly accurate as I was now 49, but no one seemed to notice. My topic, an interesting one, was "The Medical Air Evacuation System for the U.S. in Europe," which I presented in both English and French. Charlotte had driven with me, and at the conclusion of the conference we embarked on a gastronomic tour of the region.

When President Charles de Gaulle announced in 1966 that France would withdraw from NATO's military structure, he decreed all American and British bases on French soil must be closed. Most of the flight wings and squadrons were transferred from Toul-Rosières, a USAF base in the eastern part of France, to bases in Germany, many at Ramstein. As a result, during our assignment there from 1969-1973, the base population and mission increased dramatically. Ramstein Air Base became the home to the 12th Air Force and headquarters for the United States Air Force Europe (USAFE).

An expanded cargo port was built so the largest aircraft in the Air Force inventory, the C-5 and the C-141, could be used at Ramstein. All this flying activity gave me opportunities to ride on missions, usually in the jump seat of a C-130. On one trip, I flew with members of the Seventh Special Operations Squadron, also based at Ramstein. As with all SOS units, the squadron's missions were often classified. Members of the group, who were assigned their own flight surgeon, routinely disappeared for weeks at a time. I went along for a not-so-secret radar calibration flight. As we flew, ground radar units in our flight path used our location to determine the accuracy of their equipment, akin to checking the mileage odometer against signs posted on the highway. Our route took us from Ramstein through France and out over the Atlantic Ocean. From there, we reentered European air space above Spain before we flew back to Ramstein.

We visited as many places as possible during our four years in Europe, making frequent trips to Paris either as a stopover or destination. By 1970, all the family members had relocated in France. Many lived in Paris, giving us the pleasure of many reunions. Again, proximity to family was important. My parents' apartment in Antony Hauts-de-Seine was across the street from Alex and Anna Daninos' pharmacy and laboratory. To remind you of the interconnected families, Alex's mother and Aurette's mother were sisters. Anna's sister, Josette Bonan, (who

took Jean-Michel and Nicole to the Jura during the war)
lived in nearby Parc de Sceaux. This was a lovely Paris
suburb just a few kilometers from Alex, Anna, Georges
and Aurette. You get the picture.

By the time we moved to Germany, Mario and
Françoise had bought a large combination apartment
and law office on the Boulevard St. Germain. That eliminated the commute issue as they only dealt with the impossible Paris traffic when they appeared in court. Their
son, Pascal, rides or I should say, zips around Paris on
his Vespa motorcycle. No parking problems for him. His
maneuvering skills, developed from the time he was a
law student 20 years ago allow Pascal the flexibility to
use the Vespa for transport to client meetings, for court
appearances and for travel between his office and home.

Aurette and three of her five sisters lived in Paris.
Their daily phone calls and frequent get-togethers provided the links between the family branches. Their presence is sorely missed as the family has grown and in
many cases, gone to distant lands. I have relatives not
only in France, but in the Czech Republic, Turkey, Israel,
United States, and Mexico as well. Like me, many cousins have married outside the faith; however, there are
pockets of the younger generation that are observant in
Jewish culture and religion. Whatever they do, we are
proud of all and pleased to be part of this large diverse
family.

I'm getting ahead of myself with this description of family and travels. Soon after we landed in Germany, I started repeating the phrase I had been talking about for two years. "Nicole must learn to play the piano!" Never mind the only keyboard instrument we had was a Schroeder-size toy piano. We found a teacher so Nicole could start lessons, but it soon became evident we needed a real piano. At the time, we lived on the fourth floor of a Ramstein apartment building. We bought an upright for $50. It was worth what it cost.

In Europe, men were used to carrying furniture up the stairs. Bulky, oversized pieces were frequently hoisted by a crane and moved into or out of a room through a window. For our piano, two workmen strapped harnesses around their shoulders and backs, placed the piano in this sling then carried it up four flights of stairs.

Before our rotation back to the States, we discarded that clunker and bought another, equally bad, but it didn't seem to bother Nicole. Her musical talent was obvious and she progressed quickly. On one occasion, Nicole and three other young pianists were invited to perform on a local children's television show broadcast from the Armed Forces station in Ramstein. She had been told to bring two works, but when she arrived she learned there was time to play just one selection. However, since she had prepared two pieces, Nicole played both, thus cancelling the opportunity for the last child's performance. A star is a star. Happily, the little boy who had been sidelined was invited to return the following week.

I've talked about work, cars, trips and family, but I haven't mentioned the most important event of our four-year stay in Germany.

Drumroll! Cecile Juliette Narboni was born at Landstuhl Army Hospital, May 31, 1971. Our second daughter arrived without incident following Charlotte's badminton game earlier that day. Here I was, 47 years old and a new father.

Cecile fit right in, learning to travel at an early age. When she was two months old, we drove with both children to the Alabriga, our favorite Costa Brava hotel. We managed, but I don't know that I'd do that again. On the return trip to Ramstein, we made a detour to the Loire Valley area. The *Son et Lumières* or sound and light shows at the castles, particularly the one at the Château Chenonceaux, beckoned. We packed Cecile in her portable bassinet, carried her between us, and with Nicole, walked along the avenue that led to the castle. We placed Cecile's carrier on a stone wall and leaned against it as we listened to the telling of the story of French royalty and the mistresses who lived in those beautiful chateaux.

I get tired just thinking about the projects we undertook, particularly in the name of fun.

When I grow up I want to be ...

Before I close this chapter, I must let everyone know that within a year of our arrival we sold the Nash Rambler to an airman for $50. I don't feel guilty because the car worked and I continued to see it when I drove around the base.

We needed a second car so we bought a new Peugeot 504, which we picked up at the factory in Montbeliard, France. It had power steering, a radio, but no air conditioning. It certainly cost less than the Mercedes, both to buy and to maintain.

Life passed pleasantly during our stay in Germany. I note that I have not spent as much time writing about my professional responsibilities. I certainly had them, but after three years of hospital residency and the year in Vietnam I was ready to enjoy life to the fullest.

As I write this, I realize the next phase of my career and our family life together would start with a bang. I was fascinated by the changes that were taking place in the field of cancer chemotherapy and I felt I had a certain ability to care for patients with this diagnosis, so I applied for and was accepted as a postgraduate fellow at The University of Texas System Cancer Center, M.D. Anderson. In 1973, after nearly four years in Germany, we packed our belongings and prepared to move again. Charlotte was still in her "fear of flying" phase so we asked for and received authorization for sea transport, although not because of Charlotte. I can assure you the

Air Force didn't care about Charlotte's fears. We received the standard cost of transportation for military members and dependants; any additional costs were paid by us. We booked passage on the original SS *France*, the flagship of the French Line. The saleswoman at the showroom in Paris suggested the most forward cabin on the ship in tourist class. Little did we realize we would feel the movement of the ship each time it plowed through the waves. We could not stand without feeling dizzy when we were in our cabin, and so used it only for sleeping. Four berths in this small space did not make the accommodations any more appealing. Our cat fared better. His accommodations were in first class.

Picture this: We drove the cars to the departure port of le Havre, the day before boarding to check in the Peugeot and the Mercedes. The following day we went aboard with a substantial amount of luggage because we were going to be on the road for several weeks before reaching our Houston destination. In addition to our luggage, we had 22 boxes filled with china and crystal that we had purchased for friends and planned to deliver these packages at various stops as we made our way from New York to Houston via Florida. Don't forget the cat!

SEVENTEEN

....

M.D. ANDERSON HOSPITAL, HOUSTON

As we sailed into New York harbor on Cecile's second birthday, she looked over the railing and repeated several times, "Amer-eee-ca," "Amer-eee-ca!"

Yes, we were back. While we had been away, touch-tone dialing had appeared and the rotary dial phone went the way of cars with stick shift. Cable television stations were popping up, bicycles became an accepted form of transportation for grown-ups, and President Nixon would soon learn about the Watergate Hotel.

We had more pressing issues. It was June 1973 and we had to find a place to live without delay as my fellowship started July 1.

But, before we landed at our final destination, we had to address the issue of the boxes, two children, two cars and the cat. We started making deliveries. After a brief stop in Lancaster for Madalyn to meet Cecile, her new granddaughter, and marvel at Nicole's pianistic talents, we drove to Silver Spring, Maryland, where most of the boxes were handed over to our friend Dolores Early. From there, we continued to Ft. Walton Beach, Florida, to see Joanna and Warren Gourley. Warren was still on active duty at Eglin Air Force Base, and their son, Craig, the "chaud" pilot I mentioned in an earlier chapter, was in high school. Not only did we leave more boxes, we left Nicole, Cecile, the cat, and the Green Mercedes as well. That's friendship. In the summer heat, we drove the non-air conditioned Peugeot 600 miles to Houston. On this trip, we had our introduction to the humidity that makes Houston practically unmanageable in the summer. Fortunately, everything in Houston was air-conditioned, even in 1973. Stores and offices were chilled to about 65 degrees. While the first blast of cold air coming in from the outside felt great, within a minute or two the temperature would be too cold. Don't ever plan to visit a store in Texas during the summer without a jacket.

With typical Narboni determination and a little bit of luck, we found a suitable house in an area just 20 minutes from the hospital. We paid our deposit, parked the Peugeot in the driveway and flew back to Florida for the rest of the family.

Apparently, while we were in Texas, Cecile, our two-year old toddler, had been busy, breaking anything within her reach. Naptime was particularly perilous for the Gourley artifacts as Cecile was left alone in the study; instead of sleeping, she used the time to examine, play with and subsequently break a number of treasures. Did I mention Joanna was the Queen of Clean? She was famous for her organizing, decorating, and cooking skills. Charlotte always said that Joanna, whom we had met when we moved to Edwards, taught her everything she knew. Cecile, to put it kindly, upset the Gourley apple cart. Summing up the stay in Florida, when Charlotte asked Joanna whom she would prefer to have the next time, Cecile or the cat, Joanna, not a cat person, said without hesitation, the cat! Our friendship survived this traumatic period. The Gourleys remain precious friends.

Again, I was starting a new job. Here I was, nearly 49 years old and a student. While I was a fully licensed physician, an internist, and a lieutenant colonel on active duty in the United States Air Force, I was about to become a Fellow in Developmental Therapeutics at one of the world's leading cancer research and teaching hospitals. While being a fellow might not be the bottom of the rung at M.D. Anderson, it was not an exalted position either.

However, I was pleased and grateful to be part of this environment even if it meant starting close to the bottom.

I think M.D. Anderson was, is and probably always will be a special institution. Much has changed since the mid-'70s; the hospital facilities have expanded dramatically and significant progress has been made in the research and development of cancer treatment.

Like my assignment at Edwards Air Force Base 10 years earlier, it was an exciting time to be at M.D. Anderson. Many new developments and breakthroughs in research and treatment were made during this period.

Developmental Therapeutics (DT) at M.D. Anderson was a special unit separate from the Department of Medicine. DT was at the leading edge of research in developing drugs for cancer treatment. It was here that I would spend the next two years learning new therapeutic methods to manage patients with cancer.

Emil Freirich, M.D., the head of Developmental Therapeutics, was one of the world's leading cancer researchers and a genuine brilliant thinker. Many of his concepts in treating cancer have become standard practice. For instance, Dr. Freireich's idea to combine different drugs for treating cancer was not standard procedure in the early '70s. Today, combination chemotherapy is an effective part of the treatment, and certain forms of childhood leukemia are considered curable in part due to Dr. Freireich's research.

The training program at M.D. Anderson was rigorous and well defined. The day began with a conference at 8 am. The latest treatment, drug reports and specific cases were discussed. The physicians who held university appointments as assistant, associate and full professors attended, as well as the interns, residents and fellows. These meetings could be intense, as the current research and treatment plans were still under investigation and data could be disputed or questioned. Research is not for the faint-hearted. No one wants to be treated without being confident the most stringent investigation has been used.

The treatment of infectious disease was so important it had its own department. Anti-cancer drugs destroy the body's white cells as they kill the tumor. Without white cells to fight infection, a patient will develop a fever, and if not successfully treated, the effects can be catastrophic. Gerald Bodey, MD., the head of the infectious disease section, was a pioneer in this field, providing much of the clinical research used to develop effective antibiotics. Today, the treatment has evolved—the drugs are less toxic, and the side effects, including infection, can be managed successfully from the beginning of the treatment. Much of this success is due to the clinical research in the '70s and '80s.

Immunotherapy treatment for cancer was just starting when I was at M.D. Anderson. We treated melanoma with BCG, a tuberculosis culture injected into the solid tumors capable of killing cancer cells. Today, the principle remains the same, but it is a much more elaborate form of treatment. Patients can be cured using immunotherapy.

Following the morning conference, I made hospital rounds. It was my responsibility to do patient history and physicals. Back to my intern days again! I did the preliminary work, updating the lab reports, noting the results on the chart and making rounds with the attending physician.

There was usually a conference scheduled during lunch. We ate, listened and discussed cases all at the same time. Most afternoons were devoted to seeing patients in outpatient clinics. These were organized by disease. There were separate clinics for leukemia and blood-related disorders, breast cancer, lung cancer and another for GI diseases, including liver and pancreatic cancer. As in the morning, I'd follow the same routine. I saw the patient, gathered data including a history and physical, then reported to the attending physician who evaluated the patient.

How did the patients get to M.D. Anderson? The University of Texas facility was a research institution. Patients were referred by their primary care physician to the doctors in the department researching the specific type of tumor.

The treatments were tough, often resulting in hair and weight loss, infections and fever, and pain. In spite of the traumatic nature of the disease and its often-inevitable conclusion, I found working at M.D. Anderson to be an uplifting experience.

The hospital had to be staffed 24 hours a day, seven days a week. I found myself again working at night and on weekends. Really, at my age, this seemed to be a task that could be left to the younger fellows. After one year of this added assignment, I was excused from the call schedule.

Houston was not all work and no play. This was the first time we lived in Texas. What an experience! It must have been positive because here we are in San Antonio, Texas, as we have been for the past 33 years. That doesn't include the two years we lived in Wichita Falls. So far, it's been a total of 37 years. My accent may not sound like a Texas twang, but as the bumper sticker says, "I wasn't born in Texas, but I got here as fast as I could." It took me a bit longer, but I don't regret our decision to put our roots down in the Lone Star State.

Our girls were active; it was in Houston that Cecile developed her special brand of "busyness." She had a habit of disappearing, a trait that continues to this day. We might be together in a store, a park, or a museum, it doesn't matter; one minute, Cecile is in plain sight, the next she is gone.

This is not amusing to the parents of toddlers, although Charlotte, in my opinion, has always had a somewhat casual attitude about childrearing. (I won't recount the story here, but ask Charlotte why Cecile suddenly fell asleep in her high chair while we were sitting at Luby's Cafeteria.) Cecile attended the Jewish preschool program at the Congregation Beth Israel Synagogue, three blocks from our house. No large streets had to be crossed. The routine was the same every morning. I left for work and Nicole walked to her fourth grade class at the nearby public school. Charlotte drove Cecile to nursery school after Nicole had departed. Remember how I mentioned that Charlotte can never find anything. One morning when it was time to leave, she called Cecile but did not get a response. Charlotte checked with one of the neighbors who had two small boys. Cecile had not been spotted there, either. Charlotte didn't panic but she started to be concerned so she called me at work, thinking I had given Cecile a ride to the nursery school. By the time I answered the phone, Charlotte was upset that I had not called to tell her. But, I hadn't taken Cecile to school. The next step was to call Nicole's school hoping Cecile had followed her big sister. Unfortunately no. A 3-year-old girl had not come to the elementary school. By now, Charlotte was ready to call the police. Just in case, she made one more call to Cecile's nursery school. "Yes, Cecile is here. She arrived a bit early this morning." Relief replaced panic. Cecile never had an explanation. I guess she was bored. Her father had gone to work and her sister had walked to school, so Cecile did the same. Those were different times, even in a large city like Houston. Our children played outside in our quiet subdivision without supervision. Today, children cannot even wait for the school bus without an adult nearby. This is a sad sign of the times.

Nicole did well in school and continued to make progress with her piano studies. We bought a new, better-quality upright piano for her. The grand pianos came later.

In spite of Texas' size, we made road trips. The distance is 800 miles in each direction from border to border, both east to west and north to south. The terrain ranges from wetlands in the southeast corner to pine forests in the eastern portion, mountains in the far southwest, and in between open land. Texas has deserts, the Hill Country, bird sanctuaries, mountains, a large stretch of coastline along the Gulf of Mexico and plenty of oil and natural gas underground. The population has grown dramatically since we first arrived. Today, Houston is the fourth largest city in the United States, San Antonio is in seventh place, outpacing Dallas at ninth, and Austin, the state capital comes in as the eleventh largest.

I've always been a cautious man; remember the saying, "There are no old, bold pilots." My last Houston story involves the Mercedes again. It became apparent a car with air conditioning was essential for surviving Texas summers, so for a large amount of money we had air conditioning installed in the Mercedes. (Before it was installed, Nicole frequently asked us to close the windows as we arrived at her school so it looked like we had air conditioning.) It may have been dealer installed, but unlike American and Japanese carmakers, the Germans did not understand air conditioning as it is used in this country. It never really cooled properly. Only those lucky enough to be seated in the front benefited from the refrigerated air. I also thought it was a drain on the engine so I insisted it was to be used sparingly.

One hot week in July, we drove west from Houston to visit friends in El Paso. That alone will tell you how crazy we were! This was a distance of 600 miles through the hottest part of the West Texas desert. Yes, we left very early in the morning but we still had a day and a half of hard driving. I offered Charlotte and the girls one of two options: If we drove without air conditioning, we could push the pedal to 70 miles per hour. With air conditioning, we would have to keep our speed to 60 mph. It was not in dispute. We drove hundreds of miles with

When I grow up I want to be . . .

all the windows open, the girls' heads halfway outside the car and Charlotte complaining most of the way. At least we didn't have the cat!

EIGHTEEN

··

THE FINAL AIR FORCE YEARS
1975-1981

The United States Air Force moves in mysterious ways. As I was nearing the end of my two-year fellowship, I started thinking about my remaining assignments. The compulsory retirement age for active duty in 1975 was 60. If I wished, I still had eight years to serve. We enjoyed Air Force life and looked forward to one or two more assignments. By now, I could think about the probability of being promoted to full colonel and the leadership positions that would bring.

I don't remember Charlotte and I had a wish list for our next assignment, but if we were given a choice, it would be by the sea. Eglin Air Force Base, Florida, was close to the Gulf of Mexico. This fairly large hospital in Florida's Panhandle sounded like a good idea, although by this stage there would have to be an opening as either first or second in command. Officers in these jobs tended to stay longer in leadership positions, particularly if they were in attractive locales. Unless they retired or ran afoul of higher-ups they would not have to move at a set date.

Of course, there was another phone call. I was in the last six months of my stay at M.D. Anderson when a call came from the Medical Corps Personnel office asking me to visit the hospital at Sheppard Air Force Base in Wichita Falls, Texas. The Chief of Professional Services had been reassigned, code for fired, although in the Air Force Medical Corps you had to do something egregious for them to force you to retire. I don't remember his situation, but he was no longer around.

Charlotte and I looked at each other. We understood how to play the game, so of course I said yes, but mentioned that the base would not be my first choice for an assignment. Wichita Falls is about 160 miles northwest of the Dallas metroplex. It is the entrance to the Texas Panhandle and just 30 miles from the Oklahoma border. Not a drop of water in sight!

Sheppard AFB, a large training base, is the second stop on a recruit's USAF journey. After completing basic, airmen selected for technical training spend several months learning their craft at Sheppard. On any given day 15,000 people are assigned to the base. Imagine how many hospital or clinic visits that generates.

When we arrived for our initial visit, we met the senior officers who told us about the work and life at Sheppard. It was a pleasant visit since we were always open to new opportunities and friendships. Like all Air Force installations, people make the difference, but that didn't mean we wanted to relocate there. As we drove away Sunday afternoon I looked in my rearview mirror and we agreed that with any luck we would never see Sheppard or Wichita Falls again.

It was only a matter of days before I received another phone call from personnel. This time it was not a request. I was to be assigned to Sheppard as Chief of Medicine with the promise that if I found another assignment, I could leave in two years.

So, here we were, off to another part of Texas. We rented our house in Houston and found a place to rent in Wichita Falls. The town was in the middle of the Oklahoma-Texas corridor known as Tornado Alley. That should tell you about the climactic conditions. As Wichita Falls was east of the Panhandle, the winters were milder, but it was just as hot as Amarillo in the summer. There wasn't much rain, although Charlotte insists she saw it rain mud one time. When we inquired about the weather, we were told that stepping outside in summer was like "putting your head in a hot oven." The wind blew all the time, or so it seemed, and there was little natural beauty to entice visitors or tourists. During our stays in Hawaii, Europe, and San Francisco, many friends came to visit, but only one couple, Carolyn and

Tom Huff, friends from our Germany and Houston assignments and Madalyn, Charlotte's mother, came to Wichita Falls.

The topography could best be described as barren and arid. Mesquite trees, the results of cattle overgrazing, abound. This tree doesn't have much going for it except as a slow-burning wood for smoking meat. Mesquite has a stunted appearance; it provides little shade and its branches sprawl at weird angles close to the ground. Generally, the leaves appear in an unremarkable fashion, popping out of the limbs willy-nilly. I have never seen a beautiful mesquite tree. Here in San Antonio, home to its fair share of mesquite, it's used to identify the end of freezing temperatures. When the mesquite leaves start to emerge there will be no more frost.

In Wichita Falls and the surrounding area, the tumbleweed, an unattractive form of plant life with shallow roots, floats across the landscape on windy days. These thorny bushes have a life and a path of their own. There are also jackrabbits and gophers. The overpopulation of these rodents causes problems for farmers and ranchers.

My best memory of area fauna came on a hot summer day. An army of large tarantulas crossed in front of our car as we drove along a country road. They must have been four or five inches long, because their dark bodies showed up clearly on the light-colored concrete. I wish we had had a camera; it was one of those sights no one will believe unless there is photographic proof.

I've mentioned the negatives about Wichita Falls. Let me tell you about the positive. The citizens were remarkable. Anyone who chooses to live in an area that has little natural beauty or a great climate, or is far from a vibrant metropolitan area, must have a special reason and determination to remain. In this case, the incentive was oil, although ranching had started Wichita Falls' economic boom in the late 1800s.

In the early 20th century, oil changed the face of Texas. The wildcatters came from the southeast corner to West Texas and to the northwest part around Wichita Falls. For those who struck oil, the rewards were almost beyond belief. Today, the boom continues, although old-timers will tell you that there have been many busts. When a barrel of oil drops below a certain price, it's not worth the expense of exploring, drilling, and transporting this commodity. It is not a profession for the faint-hearted. Today, natural gas, as well as oil, contributes to the economic health for the region.

All this wealth created a special lifestyle for those fortunate to be winners in the oil patch. This economic generator can include the geologist, the petroleum engineer, the oil field worker, farmer or rancher on whose land the oil well is drilled, those who lease or sell the oil rig equipment, the truckers and of course, realtors, merchants, etc. Not everyone in Wichita Falls was rich, but there were many more wealthy people than we had known could exist in such a small city. Private planes and second and third homes were not uncommon. The homes of the wealthy would not have looked out of place in any upscale American neighborhood.

Charlotte resumed teaching French cooking classes in Wichita Falls. She had launched this new activity during our assignment in Germany. There, once a week, a group of eight Army wives from nearby Landstuhl Army Hospital sat in our kitchen and watched Charlotte prepare French dishes, including many recipes she had learned from my mother or another relative.

In Wichita Falls, Charlotte was introduced to the town when the Wichita Falls Museum of Art sponsored her cooking classes. The courses were popular and thanks to this introduction, we found our way into the community through French cuisine. As an aside, some of the best parties we ever attended were in Wichita Falls.

Nicole was also busy; she had been recommended to a piano teacher who, for the first time, provided the necessary technical underpinnings that had been missing in earlier teaching. Nicole still has the plaque she received after she won her teacher's Practice Contest. Today, she loves showing it to her students.

Being a teenage girl meant Nicole also loved horses, so there were weekly riding and jumping lessons as well, but we resisted making a commitment to buy a horse.

Cecile started first grade. Apart from wanting to ride a horse like her big sister, she was busy with school and her friends.

I was the Chief of Medicine at the base hospital. One evening, my immediate boss, the Chief of Professional Services, called and asked me to come to the hospital at 8 am the next morning. When I arrived, the hospital commander told me I had been selected for o-6. Further, the appointment was effective immediately. Without delay, I was suddenly a Colonel, USAF Medical Corps. My silver oak leaves were replaced with eagles and I became a bird Colonel. For those of you who are not familiar with the insignia for officers, the bird Colonel refers to the silver eagles placed on each shoulder. This promotion led to other changes. As the Chief of Professional Services was about to retire, I took that position. To round out my military credentials, I completed the School for Hospital Commanders course that was taught at Sheppard. Now I was ready for my next assignment.

Almost two years to the day after we arrived in Wichita Falls, the Clinic Commander position at Peterson Air Force Base in Colorado Springs, Colorado, became available. The Narbonis were on the move again, this time to a breathtakingly beautiful part of the country. Colorado

Springs, at an elevation of 6,000 feet, lies in the foothills of the eastern slope of the Rocky Mountains. Pikes Peak, at 12,000 feet altitude, dominates the skyline. The air is crisp and clean and the sun shines brightly most days. With Peterson Air Force Base, the Air Force Academy, the Army's Ft. Carson and NORAD, the North America Aerospace Defense Command, you could say it's a military town. It's also home to the storied Broadmoor Hotel and headquarters for the United States Olympic Center, a training site for Olympic hopefuls. Add to that its proximity to some of the best skiing in the world and it's easy to see why this is such a desirable assignment. We spent three wonderful years in Colorado Springs, meeting friends we still have 30-odd years later.

I had a good job. As commander of the Peterson Air Force Base Clinic, I was in charge of the health care services for active duty and retired personnel. After about 18 months on the job, I received another phone call asking me to take on a second assignment as ADCOM Surgeon. With the new position, I was placed in charge of medical activities for the Air Defense Command. This command, with its operations center buried deep in the rocky interior of Cheyenne Mountain, worked closely with NORAD, the North American Air Defense Command. NORAD was a joint USAF and Canadian Command, The chief officer was a Canadian Lieutenant General. Like most Canadians, the one we knew had a great personality and told very funny jokes. Even better, the general had a plane at his disposal. Although it was an old Fairchild two-engine propeller plane modified into a turboprop, it was outfitted in private plane fashion. The General spoke frequently at Air Force and civilian group meetings throughout the U.S. and Canada, so he needed efficient transportation.

He could invite guests, including wives, to travel with him on these trips. We were fortunate to be included in trips to San Diego, Tampa, and Victoria, BC. The front of the plane had regular seats, but the back had banquette seating. Alcoholic beverages, which are strictly forbidden on any U.S. military plane or ship, were served after takeoff. At mealtime, fresh linens appeared on our tables and wine was served. We thought we had arrived! Our only responsibility was to show up at the scheduled time both going and coming. At the appointed hour, we boarded, buckled up and waited for the general and his wife. As soon as they arrived, the stairs were pulled up, engines were started and the plane departed. This was a golden goose with a golden egg. Why would one want to be late?

Charlotte resumed teaching cooking classes, this time at a shop in the Broadmoor Hotel. One of her students, the wife of the newspaper publisher, suggested that Charlotte write a weekly column for the newspaper. Well, why not? For the next two years, Charlotte wrote a weekly column on food, wine, and travel. After we moved to San Antonio, she continued writing a weekly newspaper column before expanding into articles published for airline magazine.

The girls were involved with skiing and piano lessons, but riding lessons provided the most excitement. I don't know what it is about girls and horses, but Nicole never gave up her dream of having her own horse. As parents, we knew horse ownership required never-ending challenges, not the least of which were significant amounts of money needed to support an eating machine with a large body mounted on four spindly legs. We were reluctant to go down that path so we leased a horse, but the second time Nicole rode him, we realized he had a serious chronic leg injury. That took care of the lease option. On another occasion we attempted to buy a horse at auction that Nicole had ridden and liked, but the final sale price for the horse was too expensive, so we had to continue our search.

There's a conclusion to this story, but first, I have to mention Nicole's piano studies. Nicole had been accepted as a student of Reah Sadowsky, the artist-in-residence at Colorado College. It was an unlikely match. Reah Sadowsky was 62 and Nicole was 13. Their first year together was a difficult experience for both. I don't think they were speaking the same language. As a young prodigy, Reah had studied with the great pianist-teachers of the '20s and '30s. Nicole had obvious musical talent, but apart from her Wichita Falls teacher she had not had particularly good instruction. Reah taught lessons in her home, where she had installed a Baldwin concert grand piano with a lightning-fast action. The keys could be pushed down with almost no resistance. To Reah this was important, because her hands were arthritic and she could not play a piano if the keys were stiff or tight. For Nicole, without the experience and technique of a professional, it was difficult to control the keys, making lessons even more challenging. I think everyone was frustrated. After one year, just as we were starting to think about other options, something clicked! I think Reah and Nicole connected because they both had an extraordinary love of music. Suddenly they started to speak the same language. From that point, the lessons changed and the Saturday morning meetings became fun for both teacher and student—one had a great deal to learn and the other had a lifetime of musical experience to share.

Every fall the local music teachers association sponsored a competition. Reah encouraged Nicole to enter the piano concerto division even though she was just 15. The competition winner would be the soloist during the local community orchestra's fall concert. As the contest was open to all piano students up to and including college-age seniors, the deck seemed stacked against Nicole. How could she compete against 22-year-old pianists? Nicole has never been one to give up, so in spite of the seemingly insurmountable challenges, she learned Beethoven's second piano concerto for the competition.

Let's pick up the horse story again. To encourage her, we told Nicole if she won the concerto competition, we would buy her a horse.

I could go on and on, as this is one of my favorite memories, but I'll skip to the end of the story and tell you that Nicole won the competition. Were we proud parents? One evening, shortly after she won, we sat at dinner discussing her four-legged prize, not yet selected. Nicole's piano, an upright, was clearly inadequate for her level. Without much thought behind the question, we asked if she would prefer a horse or a grand piano, as buying both would not be economically possible. Nicole took about 20 seconds to make her decision. A piano! The rest is history.

As we lived in a beautiful locale, we had many visitors, including both my mother and my mother-in-law. However, one of the visits was not a happy one. Charlotte's mother, Madalyn, had been diagnosed with cancer. It had advanced somewhat so she needed radiation before surgery. Since she lived alone in Pennsylvania, we made arrangements for my mother-in-law to have the operation in Colorado Springs. After Madalyn recovered she went home, hoping for the best, but we knew there were no guarantees.

As we approached the third year in this assignment, I began to make post-Air Force plans, and with two young daughters still in school, there was no thought of retiring.

We knew our future would not include shoveling snow. Since we enjoyed Texas and Texans, I started looking for a San Antonio assignment. In the Air Force, a PCS, or permanent change of station, requires a minimum one-year commitment before retirement. It did not take long to find an Air Force position as San Antonio was home to five military bases, including Wilford Hall, the largest USAF hospital. I was assigned as Chairman, Primary Care department, a position I held until my retirement in 1981.

We began to plan our last move. We had been on the road virtually all our married life. How many career moves? Nine is about right if we don't include in-town moves. When you talk to some military personnel you learn nine is pretty paltry. We weren't complaining. Our Air Force days had been good ones.

My new assignment began in July 1980, but we had to sell our house before we could buy another house in San Antonio. Further complicating the situation, Madalyn's cancer had recurred. Everyone agreed it was better for Charlotte's mother to have her chemotherapy treatment in San Antonio. Nicole and Cecile had to start new schools by the end of August so there was no time to lose.

Rabbi Selwyn Geller, a friend from Ramstein days, was stationed in San Antonio. He invited me to stay with him while I looked for a place to live. Our parameters for buying a house were not complicated. It had to have a swimming pool; it could not be too close to the neighbors and, if necessary, could be remodeled. Did I forget anything? It had to be inexpensive. We had not yet sold our Colorado Springs house and like many American families, our assets were tied up in real estate.

In August 1980, I signed into Wilford Hall Hospital at Lackland Air Force Base. This was a return to *souvenirs du temps passé*, remembrances of times past, since I had started my career as an Air Force officer in San Antonio 18 years earlier. In my new position, I was responsible for the outpatient clinics and the administrative duties in the department. I also treated patients in medical specialty clinics, including, but not limited to, those with cancer. It was demanding work; medicine always is, but I loved helping patients. I had been a physician since 1962. I was now 57 years old, considerably older than most of the other physicians in the department. One day, a woman walked into my office, sat down, looked at me and exclaimed, "At last, someone with white hair!"

When I grow up I want to be . . .

I was put in charge of finding a house; this was done before Charlotte and the girls arrived in San Antonio. I found one that was inexpensive. It had a pool and about one acre of land so it was not up against the neighbors' walls. When I called Charlotte, who was still in Colorado Springs, we agreed that I should buy it.

I had driven the Peugeot to San Antonio. Now, it was Charlotte's turn. After saying goodbye to our friends, Charlotte drove the Green Mercedes to Texas with Nicole, Cecile, the cat and Lucia, the dog, a stray lab mix, we had acquired in Wichita Falls.

I mentioned the good parts of the house; now, it was time to mention the negatives. It was dark, dreary, and small. This was not a look Charlotte appreciated. She cried the first time she saw it from the outside. The interior was worse. I knew the house had its limitations but I believed it could be much better, mostly because I had the good sense to have an architect look at it before I signed the final papers.

Now that we had a place to live, we could concentrate on family needs. Madalyn arrived shortly after we moved. It was tough for her. She had lived alone in Lancaster County for many years and now she was with us, starting an uncertain and tough battle with chemotherapy and all it implied. Madalyn was a registered nurse; she knew the routine and she was prepared to do the maximum to conquer the disease or prolong the inevitable as long as possible.

When Nicole started high school, she discovered by taking a full schedule as a junior and two classes during the following summer session, she could graduate at the end of 11th grade. This meant she could start college one year earlier than normal. Charlotte says this is because Nicole had a mother who did not believe in free periods; there was always a class to take. Nicole, being smart and a good student, made this a belief a reality.

Cecile, who was entering the fourth grade, started riding lessons; soon, the clamoring for a horse would begin, but with the other issues confronting our family, the equestrian era had to wait. Cecile made up for it when she started and eventually had two horses, though not at the same time, plus a trunk full of ribbons from hunting and jumping competitions.

I had met a physician at M.D. Anderson who was now in a San Antonio oncology group practice, and one year after our arrival in San Antonio, I signed a contract to join an existing oncology practice.

It was time to retire from active duty in the United States Air Force. On May 31, 1981, I was released from service. I won't say it was a sad day. I had done my best. I appreciated all that I had learned in the USAF. Even Vietnam was a positive experience in my mind.

When I grow up I want to be . . .

I was ready to start another career! About six months before I turned 59, I began practicing oncology medicine full time. I would continue until my retirement at 79.

NINETEEN

....

PRIVATE PRACTICE

It seems so long ago. I retired from the Air Force at the end of May 1981, and began my new career the next day. It was a challenging practice. The patients were often very sick. Most had other medical problems as well, either as a result of the cancer and treatment or because of preexisting conditions.

In spite of these challenges for the patient and for me as the primary caregiver, I found the practice to be up-lifting, and dare I say it, sometimes even fun. I loved walking into a treatment room to meet the patient and family for the first time. It was rewarding to see them for follow-up visits and to be able to greet them like old friends. A friendly relationship and open communication was essential for their cancer treatment. We'd shake hands and make small talk. I'd ask about the family and we'd chat about the problems they had that day.

Patients seldom came alone to appointments. A family member or two or three or more, or a friend all provided extra sets of ears. Like the patient, they were able to voice concerns and ask questions.

My first responsibility was to listen to the patient! If I listened carefully, I not only heard the words they uttered, I heard the words left unsaid, and it was up to me to understand their emotional needs as an important part of their care.

An approach like this takes time. The nurses and the patients understood that on my clinic days, time stood still. The patients knew they would be sitting in the waiting room for an extended period, but they also knew when we finally got together, they were welcome to ask all the questions they wanted. I stayed until they understood their treatment options completely and how we would address the next step. It was important to identify the family member who took the lead in asking the questions. This was the person with whom I dealt. Again, having a good relationship with this caregiver smoothes the way with the other members of the family as well as the patient. It's a group effort.

I learned with time the proper way to end the appointment, to know when all the questions had been answered and the patient and family were satisfied with their visit.

With a strong patient-physician rapport, I could tell a patient difficult realities: the treatment was no longer working, that the options had been exhausted and it was time to consider the quality of life that may remain. If it was established the patient could not be cured, then it was time to introduce a strategy to manage the cancer as a chronic disease. Although we may have continued drug therapy, our treatments were focused on minimizing toxicity. We emphasized supportive care that included good nutrition, effective pain control and access and co-ordination with social services.

If the time came to consider end-of-life options, the presence of previously established trust between us helped the process. The patient often introduced the subject, and although it was not a pleasant topic, it was an important part of medical care. I think the decision to enter the hospice program often brought a feeling of relief to the patient and family. Seldom was I willing to make a statement concerning a patient's length of sur-vival. As far as predicting life or death, it was my belief one should never attempt to guess its duration.

During my years in practice, the advances in cancer treatment were significant. Today, more than 10 years since I last walked into a patient's room, the options for managing this disease have increased dramatically.

As I mentioned in an earlier chapter, while I was at M.D. Anderson, the use of immunotherapy in cancer treatment was just beginning. By the time I retired from practice in San Antonio, immune therapy was well established as an effective cancer treatment, particularly in breast cancer.

In the early '80s, nausea and vomiting were common and debilitating side effects in cancer chemotherapy. The development of better antiemetic drugs provided relief so patients could return to work and normal life even while undergoing treatment. Learning to manage pain by prescribing more liberal use of narcotics allowed patients to tolerate the effects of both the disease and the treatments. Stronger, more effective antibiotics were developed. All these advances and ongoing research, particularly in gene therapy, gave the physician greater flexibility in managing cancer.

Practicing medical oncology was a rewarding experience for me. It was a constant learning environment, both in reading about clinical research and the realities of patient treatment. The private practice physician is in the trenches when it comes to applying new knowledge for patients with complex diseases.

Some of our patients were on drug research protocols. In certain cases we would recommend that a patient go to M.D. Anderson or another research institution for diagnosis and further evaluation. Now, the situation was reversed from my fellowship experience. I would call the attending, or charge physician of the medical or surgical department researching my patient's type of cancer. An appointment was set for him or her to be seen at M.D.

Anderson or another research center. When the patient returned, we established treatment based on the hospital's recommendation. If the patient were selected for a research protocol, we monitored the care between return visits to the hospital.

I felt competent in my ability to treat patients, but I was unprepared for the hassle, the paperwork, and the bureaucracy surrounding a non-governmental practice. And, they thought the USAF was built on forms! The government is in all our lives, none more than in the practice of medicine.

Let me explain what happens when a patient seeks treatment. Keep in mind I have been retired from practice for 10 years but I've visited enough medical offices since that time to know that there isn't less paperwork, there's more!

In the 20 years I was in private oncology practice, the ability to treat patients without interference from insurance companies or government agencies diminished considerably. The rules changed frequently. I'll start with Medicare since most patients who seek medical help are seniors. The body wears out as we age, no surprise there. Cancer is a disease more prevalent in older men and women. That means most payments for services come from Medicare. You read about the government cutting payments to providers. Instead of paying what the government had agreed to pay for physicians' services the preceding year, reimbursement will be cut by 10% or more the coming year. You can be sure that private insurers match the cuts, so the physician in private practice will be paid less from that source as well. Unfortunately, the cost of drugs, the rent, employees' salaries and all the other expenses will not be cut. Most likely, they will increase.

This problem is in the news today, but it was a similar situation in 1982. We called our Medicare regional office repeatedly to ask when we could expect our payments, often waiting months to be reimbursed for patient treatments. One of our employees did nothing but call insurance companies and Medicare for prior approval before a procedure or drug treatment could be started.

The physician today is in danger of being a bureaucrat first and a caregiver after that. I would never have survived the introduction of Electronic Medical Records as I cannot type. Imagine as a physician that I have to type as I speak with the patient. I would spend all my time looking at this small keyboard rather than watching the patient.

I am concerned about the future of medicine. Here we are, with daily advances in the treatment of disease being introduced, and yet we are losing the battle to treat patients without the significant interference of the government between physician and the patient.

TWENTY

....

A LOOK BACK

My traceable family history began with the arrival of David Narboni in Algeria more than 250 years ago. For him, the journey from Livorno, Italy, must have seemed momentous and life changing. My journey started in his adopted country but it is reaching the final chapter for this memoir in San Antonio, Texas.

We were busy in the early 1980s. As I had promised Charlotte, an architect designed an addition for our house, the first of many changes we made to the property. Over the years, we renovated many times, occasionally over earlier renovations. Our house became our home. We continue to enjoy it today, more than 30 years after Charlotte first saw it.

I can't conclude this memoir without mentioning the San Antonio activities of Charlotte, Nicole, and Cecile. In addition to writing about food and wine and travel, Charlotte branched into new fields. As she likes to say, she does something different every decade. To prove this point, shortly after we arrived in San Antonio, Wilford Stapp, a petroleum engineer, and a few other committed classical music aficionados launched a 24-hour classical music radio station. Charlotte signed us up as founding members in 1982. Today, Texas Public Radio has a 24-hour NPR station as well as stations operating in Kerrville and in West Texas. After working as a volunteer for two years, Charlotte joined the board of directors and served in that capacity for several years. She eventually left the volunteer side and joined the staff, creating and managing multiple station fundraising campaigns for the next 19 years.

Nicole continued with her music studies as an undergraduate at The University of Texas at Austin. While working on her Master's degree at the Shepherd School of Music at Rice University, she met her future husband, Mark. Nicole completed her doctoral studies at Peabody Institute, part of Johns Hopkins University in Baltimore, Maryland. Nicole and Mark formed the Clinton-Narboni Piano Duo after they married, and during the next 10 years, they won most of the two-piano, piano four-hand competitions in the U.S. and Europe, including a prize that made possible their 1995 Carnegie Hall debut. In addition to performing on both continents, the Clinton-Narboni Duo recorded four compact discs, all critically acclaimed. However, after 15 years of marriage they decided to go their separate ways.

In 2006, Nicole recorded the solo piano music of the late French composer Jean Françaix. This compact disc and the piano recordings from the Duo are heard frequently on classical music radio stations worldwide.

Cecile graduated with degrees in English and Communications. Following graduation, she worked as an intern at an Austin television station before signing on as a camera operator. From there, Cecile moved to Great Falls, Montana, for her first on-camera job as the morning show news anchor. Later, she became the evening news anchor at a television station in Grand Junction, Colorado. In 2012, she took over as weekend anchor and weekday reporter for a television station in Chico, California.

Nicole, a serious and thoughtful musician and scholar with a wide range of interests, has said if she weren't a pianist, she'd want to be a physician.

That's amusing. If I had not chosen medicine, I would have been a musician.

My interest in music dates from my childhood. I always wanted to take piano lessons, but my father thought there was no time for non-scholarly pursuits. You'll remember reading about my band experience in Watertown, New York. In spite of this limited musical history, I never tired of telling family and friends that, given the proper opportunities, I would have been a great musician. By now, I considered myself conductor material, having watched hundreds of musical directors lead an orchestra from a podium.

From my lips to God's ears. Or, in this case, Charlotte's ears. I think she got tired of hearing about my armchair conducting prowess, so being Charlotte, she decided it was time to put up or shut up.

Each winter, the San Antonio Symphony held an auction to raise money for the organization. The prizes were donated by merchants and arts organizations.

Interested symphony supporters gathered and bid by silent auction for these gifts. Charlotte, the high bidder for the prize to conduct the orchestra, came home proudly and announced my upcoming performance debut, to be scheduled during the 1985 San Antonio Symphony Pops season. It's a long way from talking about conducting, particularly if one is not a professional musician, to walking out on stage. This wasn't the first time in our married life that Charlotte acted upon her impulses. She could not understand why I wasn't jubilant.

The die was cast. There were no refunds for charitable contributions. The rest of the family was thrilled. James Sedares, the Symphony Pops conductor, invited us to his home, and after dinner, gave me some conducting pointers.

When I grow up I want to be ...

Selecting the work to be performed was not difficult. It had to be a work the San Antonio Symphony musicians were prepared to perform, no matter how inadequate the direction from the podium. Fortunately, the San Antonio Symphony musicians are first rate and completely professional so I knew if I got lost in the middle of Emannuel Chabrier's six-minute work *España*, they would carry on successfully.

Charlotte ordered a baton for me. No point in going unprepared. I donned my tuxedo and with family and friends in tow prepared for this momentous event. I must say I had done many new and different activities in my life, but I never really, truly contemplated walking on stage, pretending to be a musician. I'm pleased to say everyone did his part. I didn't collapse in a heap at the podium, the orchestra members played extremely well, and the audience responded appropriately. All this for a good cause!

Naturally, there was a party after the performance. Renata Byrne, a columnist for the *San Antonio Express-News*, noted in her column the historical aspects of this concert:

> . . . Saturday night a prominent medical
> oncologist took the baton from the hands of
> James Sedares of the San Antonio Pops con-
> cert for his initial conducting debut.

Afterward, friends Linda and Charlie Winston honored Dr. Gino Narboni by inviting 40 guests attending the San Antonio Pops concert to their home. Nothing but praise was heaped on the good doctor. University of Texas at Austin student Charles Race, son of Dr. William Race, Nicole's professor of piano at the university said, "Gino did a good job for the packed house."

"Did Narboni enjoy the experience? 'It was great fun, but there was a lot of apprehension,' he said. 'It's a whole new career,' said proud wife Charlotte."

It was the end of that episode, but inspired by my still-active, Walter Mitty-inspired belief that I could be a Maestro, Charlotte came up with the idea of using a conducting class as a fundraising tool for KPAC. During a scheduled membership drive, the announcers offered listeners who pledged $120 an opportunity to take the "So You Want to be a Conductor" class with San Antonio Music Director Christopher Wilkins.

You would not believe the response. Who knew there were so many closet conductors in the area? Class size was limited to 10 so we could all receive adequate instruction and performance time. We met at a small auditorium on the appointed evening. Charlotte had arranged for a photographer to record this important event and Chris brought along five San Antonio Symphony string musicians—two violinists, one violist, and one cellist and a bass player. To start, Chris conducted a few minutes of Mozart's *Eine Kleine Nachtmusik*, explained basic conducting technique, then listened as we, in turn, mounted the podium. After each of us took our turn, Chris made suggestions, offered comments and praise and gave us an opportunity to play the music again. The musicians treated us kindly, although you could see smiles lurking at the corners of their mouths as they were being given instructions that seldom made musical sense.

A reception followed, photos were taken and a great musical evening came to an end.

There is actually one more conducting story. I believe strongly in the power of music, so in 2007, Charlotte, Nicole, Cecile and I established The Gino R. Narboni Endowed Presidential Scholarship in Orchestral Conducting at The University of Texas at Austin, where for many years, Charlotte served on the Fine Arts Advisory Council and chaired the Music Committee. Even if I've missed the conducting train, we can help fuel the engine for someone in the coming generation.

Some concluding thoughts about my life's journey . . . First, let me say that I have been extremely fortunate. Mine is the archetypical immigrant story. I arrived in America with $500 in my pocket, joining a line that included millions of men and women from around the world with similar hopes and dreams.

From the very beginning as a French cadet pilot learning to fly in the United States, I understood the spirit of this country. It's that spirit I have always admired. Americans are not perfect, but for me, as a naturalized citizen, they are a wonderful blend of cultures, ideas, imagination, and kindness. Most of all, it's the inherent compassion of Americans I admire. I look at the photos taken of our class at Selfridge, Michigan, where we spent our final months in pilot training. I mentioned earlier an American woman regularly invited the French cadets for Sunday lunch. Imagine a group of young men, far from home during wartime, being offered a home-cooked meal. As I write this, I am reminded that during the Allied campaign in North Africa, my mother sent us to invite British officers for lunch. I shall have to expand my opening statement about Americans. Good people are good people, worldwide.

Pierre qui roule n'amasse pas mousse. A rolling stone gathers no moss. I proudly dictated this phrase to Charlotte, who with a certain amount of glee, informed me this phrase is well-known in English and she would be reluctant to give the French the right of first use. It does not matter; the idea is the same in all languages. In my case, I did gather moss in spite of rolling a long, long way. One imagines that to roll, one goes downhill. My

path has taken me up and down many hills. This journey, even on the difficult paths, has been interesting and
fulfilling.

I gained an American family and reconnected with
my French-Jewish heritage. I was the first of the Narbonis to immigrate to the new world. I can still remember my early visits "back home" to see my parents,
brothers, cousins and aunts and uncles. In the 1950s and
1960s, I was regarded as a special case: daring, original
and perhaps a bit crazy. Who would want to go to the
United States? Certainly, my family admired the Americans, but they were certain the culture would be so foreign, so wanting without good wine or cheese there
would be no reason to even visit, much less live there.
Count their reaction to Charlotte during her first visit as
part of this phenomenon. She was impossibly young, her
French language skills were limited, and because of her
inability to join the conversation, she spent most family
repasts admiring the ornate ceilings, a feature of so
many apartments. When Charlotte wanted to join the
conversation, she had to ask me to translate. The response had to be translated as well. Long, long meals,
discussing family gossip and achievements were of little
interest to a young, pregnant American who wanted to
see the sights. Charlotte, although an admirer of all
things French, including me, I'm pleased to say, found
some of their habits hard to understand. She watched

my mother struggle to eat potato chips with a fork and knife at a formal luncheon. That was in 1963, when Europe was still adapting to the postwar period of growth. They were discovering American foods, culture and way of life. Most of their information came through television programming.

The French had *pommes frites* and the Americans had French fries. Here, I'll wear my American hat; we also had large gas-guzzling cars made for touring with the entire family, modern highways and lots of accessible parking. Many, including us, dreamed of owning a home. France was still digging out from nearly a 50-year period of devastating wars and I'm including World War I in this assessment. The American amenities we took for granted seemed foreign and unattainable to the French.

The differences between the French and American cultures at the beginning of my life in the U.S. were both economic and philosophical. It was like seeing two sides of the coin. In France, I'd have countless conversations with my relatives, and in this country I'd hear the American perspective about the French. In both sets of discussions, each side presented their idea of the best and the worst of each other's country so I found myself defending one side of the Atlantic when I was on the opposite shore. For the French, the idea of not being able to buy a good cheese or wine in the states or find a good café au lait would be a deal-breaker. Most of my

American friends believed the French were stuffy, impossibly formal, and haughty to the point of rudeness. On certain points they could agree. For instance, the French still line up outside movie theaters to see new US made films and Americans admire all French culinary achievements.

Today, I have to reverse the last statement. The culinary scene in this country has exploded and most of the results are positive. I think we, speaking as an American, can hold our heads high when we discuss food and wine. Every day, chefs, bakers, wine makers and yes, food truck owners push the envelope to develop and offer delicious offerings to a knowledgeable American clientele.

We have an opportunity to watch French films thanks to Netflix and the Internet, and no one does comedy better than the French.

This *mélange* and hands-across-the-sea attitude developed, in my opinion, because of global communications. My parents came to the States once. That was a challenging adventure, given their age and attitudes. My father thought there was no need to travel internationally since everything of value could be found in France, an attitude shared by many, if not most of his countrymen.

Mario and his wife, Françoise, ventured to New York on the occasion of my 75th birthday, 15 years ago. Their son Pascal, who was 20 at the time, showed up in San

Antonio in 1981. During the next 20 years, many cousins in his age group came to see us, usually as part of a "see America tour." It was the children and grandchildren of my contemporaries, the first to venture in any significant number across the Atlantic, who opened the gates to better understanding and appreciation for life in both countries. Today, it's a rite of passage for the younger cousins and absolutely obligatory for any university-aged student. I'll bet I could not find anyone in our family under 30 who has not been to the United States.

Travel is broadening. How can you keep your closely guarded prejudices against the unknown when you know with all your senses the smelly cheese is delicious, the barbeque is outstanding and attitudes that seemed stuffy may just be a natural reticence attached to good manners?

Today the French wear jeans everywhere, even with *le smoking,* or formal jacket, but there are caveats. The jeans have to be American-made. I beg forgiveness on the issue; in spite of Charlotte and the girls having made multiple attempts to put me in denim, it has never worked. You cannot teach this old Frenchman that new trick.

Americans have learned to speak French. When I first arrived on this side of the Atlantic, I was convinced that French language studies in U.S. schools provided minimal skills, at best. In typical French fashion, or as Charlotte would say, Gino-fashion, I did not hesitate to say I would never embarrass a high school French teacher by speaking French to her/him. That, too, has changed. I have met many Americans who speak the language beautifully. Again, the walls have come tumbling down!

As long as I am musing about the differences and similarities between my native country and my adopted homeland, I cannot close without mentioning French driving style. (We can save highways and traffic pattern differences for another time.) To me, driving is an activity that requires 100% attention. I don't eat or drink while I'm driving, I don't talk on the phone and I can't text. Even conversation has to take second place to the absolutely vital task at hand, getting from one place to the next without placing my passengers or other cars and their human contents at risk.

If you have ever spent any time on a French street or highway, you will know where I am going with this. My mother, I am convinced, either did not see or simply took the white lines outlining lanes on a thoroughfare as a guide, not necessarily essential to maintain one's path. It was scary to drive through Paris with her. Charlotte refused to ride in the front passenger seat when Aurette was at the wheel. The small Simca she drove showed signs of multiple encounters with other cars and unmovable objects—curbs, etc. She was a past master at the French favorite, parking on the *trottoir,* or sidewalk. Taken one step further, Aurette was not above driving on the sidewalk to create a space that in America would earn the driver a hefty fine. She was not alone in her driving technique; this was standard operating procedure for most French drivers. No wonder that when she visited us in America, she marveled at the polite American drivers –mentioning that she heard none of the vicious insults such as those hurled by insensitive Frenchmen in Paris, no honking of horns or aggressive gestures.

No chapter on driving or parking can be complete without describing the parking techniques of our dear cousin, Jean-Michel Daninos. Sadly, Jean-Michel passed away in 2012 at the age of 70. We had many wonderful occasions together over the past 50 years. Jean-Michel, an endocrinologist, was known and loved by his colleagues and his friends. He was a Renaissance man. In the early part of his career, Jean-Michel hosted a radio show. He wrote a book about diabetes and he was a mover and shaker in his medical circle. Most of all, J-M was great fun and extremely kind and thoughtful.

We always looked forward to our time with Jean-Michel. He liked fast cars; his Porsche being his favorite, but the make didn't really matter. J-M's specialty was finding a place to park where none existed. Red or yellow lines, the corners of a busy intersection, and of course, the *trottoir* were all available to Jean-Michel as parking spots. We'd arrive at a restaurant around nine pm. As this was dinnertime for the French, there were no empty spaces. J-M's favorite location was the rounded corner of an intersection, reserved as a pedestrian crossing. It was always available since it was strictly forbidden for parking. He'd stop, park, lock the door, and enter the restaurant knowing his car was safe from harm. Yes, the caduceus displayed in his windshield gave him some protection from the fear of towing, but I'm convinced that even without the special medallion, Jean-Michel would have happily considered this an available space.

It is reassuring to arrive at this age and still have reasonably good health. It is even more rewarding to know my life is special, not because of anything I have done to make it so, but because I've been surrounded by a marvelous family, including Charlotte, my beloved wife of 50 years, and my two wonderful daughters, Nicole and Cecile. My brothers, Mario and Yvan, my late parents, and all my aunts, uncles and cousins are so important to me. I know they, along with our friends, have made it possible for me to enjoy this journey. Certainly, I thank God for giving me the opportunity to tell my story.

TWENTY-ONE

....

NINETY YEARS, PLUS . . .
CHARLOTTE NARBONI

We began this project to put Gino's life story on paper at the beginning of his 90th year. By November 18, 2013, we had accomplished our mission with the release of *When I Grow Up, I Want To Be . . .* Now, as I write this, three and a half years have passed since his 90th birthday.

Gino marked the entrance into his 10th decade with four days of festivities for friends and family. The release of his memoir formed the cornerstone for this celebration. In the weeks before his birthday, Gino spent considerable time signing books for the guests.

When we started to plan this special celebration, we asked Nicole to play a recital in honor of her daddy's special day. She agreed, as Nicole was always pleased to speak musically for her father. The weekend events were built around the musical tribute. Friends and family, including four cousins who flew to San Antonio from Par-

is, gathered for two days of activities before the official
Sunday celebration. It was similar to Texas wedding festivities, with multiple activities for the out-of-towners.
On Friday we hosted a barbeque. Saturday was set aside
for sightseeing. That evening our guests dined at a Mex-
ican restaurant. Sunday Brunch kicked off the official
celebration. This was followed by a photo session along
the banks of the San Antonio River with the guest of
honor and the out-of-towners.

The starting time for Nicole's afternoon recital was
set by California friends Margaret Ann and Lowell
Suckow, who could not arrive before midday. Margaret
Ann made it clear when she heard about the birthday
weekend: "Nicole cannot put one finger on the keyboard
before 3:00 PM!"

It was a program designed for classical music lovers.
Nicole chose Gino's favorite composers, Beethoven and
Brahms. She opened the program with the Beethoven
Variations and Fugue in E-flat Major, op. 35, also known
as the Eroica Variations. This 30-minute work was fol-
lowed by another musical monument, the Variations and
Fugue on a Theme by Handel, op. 24, by Johannes
Brahms. No easy listening, just beautiful music, a gift
from Nicole's heart.

It was time for cake and champagne, but not before
everyone toasted Gino's milestone and sang Happy
Birthday. As his mother used to say, "*Tout finit par la*

chanson." Everyone sings at the end. Before they departed, we gave our guests signed copies of the memoir.

The great day arrived! Monday, November 18, 2013, Gino's 90th birthday. The out-of-town guests spent the morning on a San Antonio River boat tour. We invited several dozen guests to our friend Jeff Glass's beautiful home that evening for the birthday dinner. Naturally, there was Gino's favorite, couscous, the all-in-one meal I mentioned in an earlier part of the book. Any important occasion in Gino's life that involved food, would by necessity, include this North African staple. Isabelle Bonan and Nicole Daninos, our French cousins, hand-carried boxes of Algerian desserts, some of which they made themselves and others they purchased at a neighborhood Arab patisserie in Paris. Dripping with honey and sugar syrup, laden with crushed pistachios and almonds, the cookies and sweets had been deep fried before being rolled and covered with the crunchy nuts. The pastries completed Gino's version of the ideal dinner. I think everyone enjoyed it even though most had never tasted North African cooking before. It is a small world, without borders, when a Sephardic Jew from Constantine, Algeria, serves a traditional Arab dinner in the heart of South Texas.

Certainly, it was a weekend and a birthday to remember.

In the midst of all this revelry, Gino was dealing with serious health issues, including recently diagnosed prostate cancer and his ever-present, albeit slow-progressing, advanced kidney failure. As so often happens when one ages, Gino also developed an inner-ear balance problem, compounded by total hearing loss. This made walking difficult. The treatment for the prostate cancer and subsequent loss of strength and mobility did not stop him from getting out and about, and our travels continued in spite of these handicaps. Gino's health was further complicated by a hip fracture he sustained in July 2015. This did not stop Gino from boarding a previously planned trip to France two months later. Excellent care, successful repair of his fracture, diligent physical therapy and a never-give-up attitude kept Gino looking forward. Prior to this accident we had been on the road with a certain determination that often took us to less-familiar places, including India and Egypt, almost always with a Paris stop thrown into the itinerary.

With the added health issues, we changed our travel style. Land-based trips stopped, apart from our California visits to Cecile and trips to Paris. Instead, we relied on cruise ship travel. Of course, we did it with a vengeance, signing up for five trips between November 2013 and May 2016. I'm not sure if we sailed the seven seas, but we traversed a significant number of them as our cruising adventures included departures from Mumbai, Bali, Fort Lauderdale, Dubai and Rome.

Cruising itineraries marked Gino's return to Israel. On the first of three separate trips to the region, Gino and I docked in two separate Israeli ports, Ashdod and Haifa. How much had changed in his first visit in 60 years? According to Gino, the same hustle and bustle he remembered from the late '40s and '50s still existed. He found the growth and development of the country exciting. There were many highlights, all new to me. Even for Gino, some of the stops, including the visit to the Western Wall, had not been part of the Jewish landscape in 1950. In the original partition that granted Israel statehood, Jerusalem was supposed to be declared international, but in the ensuing War of Independence, the Old City of Jerusalem and East Jerusalem remained in Jordanian hands. That changed after the 1967 war with the Arabs, the Six Day War; a war that started in June of that year. Israel acquired East Jerusalem from Jordan, the Sinai Peninsula and Gaza from Egypt and the Golan Heights from Syria. Today, Israel controls all of Jerusalem, although there is still an Arab quarter in the city.

On our first visit, we drove to the Golan Heights, an area that Gino had known from the time of his stay at Rayak Air Base in Lebanon. The Golan is a beautiful spot, strategically placed with the high ground now in Israeli control. There is a United Nations controlled buffer area between Israel and Syria. Checkpoints are in place and little access is granted to individuals crossing to the other side. From the viewing points on the high ground, we could look across irrigated fields planted with fruit trees and other crops. It was a beautiful sight, in spite of the turbulence of its history.

With our guide, we crossed the river Jordan (really just a small body of water) then stopped for lunch in a Druze restaurant not far from the Golan Heights.

Here we were, having lunch in a restaurant run by Arabs with a Jewish tour guide. I only wish I could return and recreate this scene as I remember it: noisy families all eating and drinking and enjoying life. Waiters delivered multiple platters of meats and vegetables, as they were prepared. There did not seem to be a strict definition of courses. When it was ready, it was served. Beverages were water and soft drinks. No iced tea and no wine or beer. As observant Muslims, the Druze do not drink alcohol. I doubt it was even available for sale.

It seemed like a simple menu. Our guide ordered the standard appetizer: olives and hummus. Not very unusual . . . except that the hummus was the best we ever tasted. I cannot tell you how many times Gino and I discussed this plate of ground chickpeas, seasoned and crushed to a smooth paste, perfumed with garlic, salted, and dotted with a healthy portion of olive oil. There were other courses; I can't remember much because I'm still overwhelmed by the memory of the hummus and olives. There would have been a salad of tomatoes and onions and garlic, chopped and presented as a first course along with the hummus and olives. For dessert, I know we had the local version of Baklava and very strong, black coffee prepared by pouring boiling water over coffee beans ground to a powder. Must add sugar!

I may have heard the word "Druze" prior to our visit to Israel but I had no real concept of this unique Arab sect. Following that visit and our lunch at the Druze restaurant, I wanted to learn more about this group, their beliefs and history with the Jewish state. The Druze sometimes support Israel politically, and Druze men even serve in the Israeli Defense Forces. The Druze, many of whom live in the Golan region, are industrious; they send their children to school and the women serve in positions of responsibility in their tribal councils.

On this same trip we visited the Scroll of Fire, created as a memorial by noted Polish-born sculptor Nathan Rapaport. The two large scrolls in the Forest of the Martyrs commemorate Jewish history from the Holocaust until Independence. In a separate forest, we paid homage at Har Hatayasim Pilots' Memorial, which commemorates the six pilots of two planes that crashed nearby during the Maccabi operation in the 1948 War of Independence. These outdoor monuments serve as a reminder of the sacrifices made by so many to accomplish the goal of a Jewish state.

On our second trip to Israel, our guide took us to the Western Wall, an essential pilgrimage for most Jews. Our visit to this site was tightly organized by the state and followed the tenets of Orthodox Judaism. Men and women are separated before approaching the famous wall. This area is all that remains from the destruction of the Second Temple, pulled down by the Romans in 20 AD.

I suspect everyone brings their personal feelings as they touch the stones. As a non-Jew, I found it compelling, an extraordinarily moving experience. Most of us are familiar with the act of leaving messages for God in the stones with the idea that He shall hear our prayers in this holy place. As our experiences were different, I was never sure if Gino left a note. He was 91. For him, just getting to a place where he could sit would override any other task. I suspect that approaching and touching the wall would have been the most important part of his visit. I, on the other hand, not being bound by religious beliefs, acted as I do in most situations: if a little is good, more is better, so I left five notes. I'm not sure if my entreaties were answered; I can't even remember what I asked for; the wishes are always the same, children and health. Nothing else has significant value for me. I gave up on world peace a long time ago. As I mentioned in earlier chapters, Gino's connection to his Jewish heritage was limited to fasting and attendance at Yom Kippur services, a practice he abandoned after the girls and I were seriously injured in a car accident in 2007. I don't think he ever forgave God for allowing this to happen. Gino's commitment to his Jewish heritage never wavered but his faith suffered at times.

We spent the morning in Jerusalem's Old City, treading the same uneven, worn-smooth stones that have been part of history for two thousand years. This is an ancient and revered place divided into four quarters: Jewish. Arab, Christian and Armenian.

Sightseeing is tiring. Breaks are essential. And sometimes these interludes can provide unforgettable moments. In the Arab section of Jerusalem, we passed vendors selling wares out of shops that were probably no more than eight feet wide and an equal number of feet deep. As we walked through the narrow passageways, darkened from the closeness of the buildings on either side, a young boy approached carrying a tray filled with plastic glasses of freshly squeezed pomegranate juice. Truly, it was manna, or at least a liquid version of this biblical food. In my memory, it was nectar from the gods. I did not see the production, but there are only a few ways to get juice from hard-cased fruit. The pomegranates had to be cut apart and the seeds scraped from their yellow honeycomb bed before the liquid could be squeezed or pressed, probably through a food mill, into a simple glass of juice. The shopkeeper of this fruit stand probably prepared the pomegranates with the same or similar technique that had been used for centuries.

Since that autumn visit, I've tried unsuccessfully to find pomegranate juice that tasted as sweet and as delicious as we encountered in Jerusalem. Two years later when we returned to Israel during the month of May and searched for fresh juice, sadly, we learned it was too early in the year for pomegranates.

Also on this visit, we took another trip down Gino's memory lane with a visit to Tel Nof, an Israeli Air Base not far from Tel Aviv. It was named Ekron after the British left Palestine and it was from Ekron that Gino departed for his daily flights to and from Eilat as a Captain in the Israeli Air Force and later as a pilot for Arkia Airlines.

Our Tel Nof adventure was not easy to arrange as all military facilities in Israel are closed to civilians, especially foreigners. However, Gino's history as a Machal and with the request from the founder of the World Machal organization, Smokey Simon, we were granted permission. We had to submit our passports and provide additional identification, including the car's license plate number and name of the person driving us to the base. In these situations, since it was to visit an air force facility, no matter the distances covered or the upheaval from his normal routine, Gino was happy. He loved being around planes and flying personnel.

We were driven to a hangar, large enough for just one or two planes. Gino was welcomed by the base commander, a pilot, who explained the mission, particularly as it applied to the lethal-looking F-15 that served as the commander's backdrop. Although Gino's gait was slow, his mind was alert; he listened intently, content and happy in an element that was for him still fresh after more than 70 years. Although we could not take photos, the base public affairs representative provided us with those they took. We later used one of these photos in an article entitled "Flying Under Three Flags," a story written about Gino for the Jerusalem Report by Bernard Edinger.

Speaking of Bernard, we have kept in contact with him since Gino's cousin, Frederic Castel, also a Paris-based journalist, introduced them 10 years ago. It was Bernard who first introduced the concept of the "Machal" to Gino. In the process of writing the memoir, Bernard opened many doors as we began the search for dates and events that had been lost through time.

In 2014, Bernard told us about the movie that Hollywood producer Nancy Spielberg and her director, Roberta Grossman, were filming. The true story revolved around three American WWII fighter pilots who were recruited to fight for Israel during the initial 1948 conflict. The film, *Above and Beyond*, was received with fanfare worldwide. Today, this true story is available on film. In San Francisco, Gino, Cecile, and I attended the North American premiere, part of that city's Jewish Film Festival. The movie brought back many memories for Gino even though as a "heavy," or bomber pilot, he had not been involved in direct combat like the three men featured in the film.

Gino and I later attended the San Antonio Jewish Film Festival screening of Above and Beyond in 2015. At a Q & A following the showing, Gino shared his story with the audience. Microphone in hand, he discussed his role during that critical period in Israel's history. There were lots of questions from audience members, and even though more than 60 years had passed, Gino gave thoughtful, cogent answers as he recalled the realities of life in a new country already under attack for its survival.

Gino was never particularly comfortable in the limelight and as he aged, his voice lost significant strength. He always worried when he could not remember names or dates but when it came to planes, he never forgot. The name, type, and country of origin could be announced with more certainty than the dates of his daughters' birthdays. Gino always made the correct identification: it did not matter if it was parked in a hanger, visible to the eye overhead, or in some cases, the noise coming from an overhead engine!

Following the question and answer session, Gino signed copies of his memoir. Long-forgotten memories were reintroduced into our lives following the publication of *When I Grow Up, . . .* all of them pleasant and some quite surprising. As Gino signed copies, a man approached and introduced himself as a cardiologist. He reminded Gino that he had referred a patient with cancer to him 25 years earlier. The woman is still alive today. According to the cardiologist, she and he both credited Gino with saving her life. To bring the story full circle, he purchased a signed copy of the memoir for their shared patient from long ago. You cannot imagine the pleasure a story like that brings to a physician, particularly after a quarter century has passed.

The memoir generated many calls, letters, and remembrances from people Gino had encountered over a lifetime. Friends called, friends of friends wrote; it continues to this day. On our final Paris visit in 2016, we met Dr. Jacques Hamou, a physician who had been an intern at Nassau Hospital, Long Island, during the period that Gino served as a resident prior to entering the USAF in 1962. Their lives never intersected again until last spring.

As I mentioned in the opening of this final chapter, we continued our "road trips" although they usually involved flying great distances to reach our cruise departure port. Gino agreed to these ambitious voyages because he would do anything to make me happy and because I managed to get him to the port in fine style thanks to careful planning and airline miles. All I had to do was wave an itinerary in front of him that included flying aboard a giant Airbus A380 and he was on board, figuratively and literally. In retrospect, I don't think I've ever seen him smile more broadly, apart from watching his daughters, than when he was on a beautiful plane. When you're in the first-class cabin aboard the Qantas non-stop flight between Dallas and Sydney, the 17-hour journey (at the time, the longest commercial flight) seemed to pass very quickly. "What, we're already there?" was our feeling as we watched the landing from our television monitor. We stayed behind to visit the cockpit crew and took some memorable pictures that still bring me pleasure.

On that trip down under in 2014, we arrived for our cruise, (after flying from Sydney to Benoa, Bali, and spending two days acclimating our bodies to the other side of the world) to learn that we had been upgraded aboard the Seabourn *Odyssey*. For travelers who play the airline and cruise game, "upgrade" is a magical word. Yes, we had received nice benefits as frequent cruisers and flyers, but on this particular voyage the accommodations were outstanding! We hadn't gotten the news about the upgrade prior to our departure so we had no idea they had placed us in one of the largest suites on the ship, complete with salon, two bathrooms, king-size bed, multiple closets, and a private balcony and deck. Best of all, as they led us from our booked suite (all accommodations aboard this cruise line are called "suites") the housekeeper opened the door into a foyer. Yes, an entrance hall. I knew I wasn't in Kansas anymore.

It took about five minutes to come up with my favorite words: "Let's have a party!" It was December, and we would celebrate our 52nd wedding anniversary during our cruise from Benoa to Sydney. Aboard Seabourn, all things are possible, even last minute wedding renewals. Invitations were sent, the menu planned, and the music arranged. As we sailed along the northeast Australian coast, Captain Mark Dexter led us in a simple, but lovely ceremony renewing our marriage vows. There were photos, a video, a few tears, and many toasts as our 40 new friends, staff members, and crew joined us for this memorable occasion.

Our lives, for the nearly three years Gino lived after his 90th birthday and the publication of the book, were filled with family, friends and travels. And there were many memorable experiences, like the Tel Nof visit. Some were small and some more public. All were meaningful to Gino.

Two years later in May 2016, we were on the road again via the A380, this time the Emirates version, again in the first class cabin, non-stop from Houston to Dubai. Same aircraft, different company and direction, but a once-in-a-lifetime flight experience for both of us. From our landing in Dubai's international airport to our departure aboard Seabourn *Sojourn* three days later, we began a 20 day cruise with stops in Israel and concluding with a memorable family reunion in Paris.

As I finish this story, I am reminded about these truths. I loved Gino for so many reasons. It's hard to count the ways; maybe, because I always believed that Gino made me who I am today and for that I shall always be grateful. One does not become a successful pilot, physician, commander of others without having a strong core and determination to accomplish a mission. Add to that his passions that endured a lifetime: his family, his patients, and flying. In fact, when we were writing the first edition of the memoir, it was only then that I realized some of his happiest moments came when he was near a flight line or in the air above.

With this project, we looked back and remembered the good times of Gino's early life and our lives together with our children, our families and our friends. In many instances Nicole, Cecile and I, as well as countless family and friends helped rebuild the stories of Gino's life. I am

When I grow up I want to be . . .

amazed that Gino's accomplishments continue to be of interest to others. It is a testimony to his character.

I have loved sharing Gino's stories.

.

TWENTY-TWO

....

POSTSCRIPT

We always knew it would end. As with other momentous events in his life, Gino left quietly and with as little fuss as possible.

The beginning of the end began July 12, 2016, just four days after our return from visiting friends in Maine. Gino developed a persistent cough that evening; by morning it was clear he needed treatment. With some cough suppressants and antibiotics he improved slightly, but by that evening the cough had returned and we took him to the emergency room. After one of those awful overnight stays that seem to go on forever, Gino was admitted to the hospital. He was placed on oxygen and received respiratory therapy, which provided some relief. Throughout the day his mind was clear, but he was obviously in distress. Knowing he was to remain in the hospital for another night, and not wanting to leave him alone, but to give me some relief, our friend Nickey McCasland spent the evening with him, and Nicole came for the night. When I returned to the hospital Friday morning, July 15, I realized his condition had deteriorated overnight. Although he was responsive, I knew Gino would not recover. After talking with Nicole, Cecile and the physicians, we made the decision to place Gino in hospice care and to bring him home.

Cecile began the trip from California. Nicole and our son-in-law, Heath, waited with Gino at the hospital until the ambulance transported him home later that afternoon. We had placed the hospital bed in the center of the living and dining room area so he could look out and see the summer foliage and trees in both the front and back gardens. Frankly, it made us feel better, but Gino's breathing difficulties overwhelmed any thoughts he may have had about the setting. The hospice nurse came that evening to help us organize for the night. Cecile's plane was late. She arrived shortly before midnight, but he had spoken his last words an hour earlier when suddenly he said, "I'm dying." All of us were with Gino when he gently took his last breath shortly after midnight, July 16.

It had taken all his energy to breathe that day despite the medication, and he had spoken little. His final words, shortly before he lapsed into unconsciousness, seemed to express both a sense of regret and wonder. How many patients had Gino seen at this point in their lives? Now it was his turn.

Although it was an extraordinarily sad moment, all of us felt a certain relief in knowing that he was no longer suffering. We had made the right decision to bring him home so we could be together as we had always been.

I wanted Gino to have a departure reflecting all the other important occasions in our life, one simple but carefully prepared. He was to be buried at Ft. Sam Houston National Cemetery, a final resting place reserved for members of the armed forces who receive honorable discharges and their spouses. The two-week delay for the scheduled July 29, 2017, interment allowed friends and family time to travel to San Antonio.

Gino was not an observant practitioner of his Jewish faith but I knew he wanted to be buried as a Jew. A friend, Dr. Michael Ozer asked Aryeh Scheinberg, the Orthodox rabbi at San Antonio's Congregation Rodfei Sholom, if he would officiate. Rabbi Scheinberg said it would be an honor to conduct the services as he recognized and valued Gino's involvement in Israel as a Machal.

It seems odd to say, but it was one of the best funerals I have ever attended. It was sad and there were tears, but there was so much warmth and personal acknowledgement of Gino's life that our family will always remember this day as a fitting tribute to him.

You never know who will attend a life event like this. In Gino's case, former colleagues, friends, caregivers and family members came to celebrate and remember this remarkable yet unassuming man. Some spoke to us, others simply signed the memory book.

On the day of the funeral my niece from Florida, Shaina Markulin, joined Nicole, Cecile, Heath and me in the family room before the service. Rabbi Scheinberg asked me if I had any special request for readings at the graveside service. We settled on the 23rd Psalm, a favorite of mine.

Nicole, in an act of bravery and love, had volunteered to perform at her father's funeral. A recipient of the Gino R. Narboni Endowed Presidential Scholarship in Orchestral Conducting at U.T. Austin and a pallbearer, James Welsch, had written a short piano composition, "In Memoriam Gino." Nicole opened the service with this solo. She closed the ceremony with the Adagio Cantabile from Beethoven's Pathetique sonata.

In one of those serendipitous moments that give life extra meaning, Rabbi Scheinberg, looking for additional information about the Machal, contacted a friend in Jerusalem. The friend, when he asked the name of the Machalnik in question, realized that he had met Gino. Yehezkel Caine, M.D., as a young Israeli pilot-physician, had met Gino during a visit to NORAD headquarters in Colorado Springs 37 years earlier. When the Rabbi recounted his conversation with Dr. Caine, we realized we had been treated to a new and lovely story from Gino's life.

Nicole and Cecile shared Daddy stories and long-time friend and fellow United States Air Force Medical Corps officer, Jack Saylor brought back memories of Gino's special qualities, including his English pronunciation quirks.

At the cemetery there was a simple but eloquent graveside service. Rabbi Scheinberg recited the prayers for the dead. An Air Force bugler played Taps and the honor guard rendered a three-gun salute. At the close of the military ceremony, I was presented with the flag that draped Gino's coffin. In accordance with Jewish law, Gino was interred in a wooden coffin. Rabbi Scheinberg presided over the committal ceremony with the required minion of 10 Jewish men. Finally, Gino was laid to rest. Il a *replié ses ailes.* He has folded his wings.

A FEW OF HIS FAVORITE THINGS

It may seem strange, but after he had taken his last breath, Cecile, Nicole, Heath and I sat by Gino's bedside waiting for the hospice nurse to return. We used the time to plan a Gino-style menu for those who would come back to the house after the funeral.

No one seemed to mind the quirky menu, and I know Gino would have loved it. Our choices may not have made culinary sense, but they were his favorite things. On the day of the funeral the caterer set up a frying station to prepare fresh, crisp French fries for the guests. Earlier that morning the French baker from Gino's favorite boulangerie delivered mini-croissants, fresh baguettes and a chocolate cake. Platters of sliced ham, crudités, and his favorite cheeses; Brie, Camembert, Tommes Crayeuse, Roquefort, and Gruyere were part of the table display. There was French red wine and champagne. A box of handmade chocolates was sent specially from Maine as a gift from our friends and neighbors the Carolins. I had ordered sticky, sweet, honey-filled Middle Eastern pastries from the same company in Michigan that had supplied them for Gino's 90th birthday celebration. Cecile hand carried a crate of fresh, ripe figs, a gift from Bob Steinacher, the owner of a commercial fig farm. We had met Bob on an earlier visit to California after Cecile had profiled him for a story on the local television station.

Our longtime friends Joanna Gourley and Carolyn Huff, came a day before the funeral to help. They set the table and performed the tasks that we had done for many other occasions, though none so sad and final as this one. As always, Joanna and Carolyn performed them with love. Our friend Suzanne Pack was there, helping with planning, creating the special memory books and serving as photographer, giving us images to hold close for many years to come.

Those who came to the collation enjoyed the afternoon, many of them staying to talk about Gino, recounting stories and times they had shared with him. Like so many of our gatherings, this one had a mixture of young and not-so-young friends, work colleagues, caregivers and neighbors.

It was a warm and loving tribute to Gino, as we honored the memory of our dear husband, father, uncle, friend and colleague.

I finish these pages with the words of his beloved daughters, Nicole and Cecile; his good friend Jack Saylor; and the remarks provided by Yehezkel Caine, M.D., who met Gino just once 37 years ago but remembers him to this day.

WORDS FROM NICOLE AURETTE NARBONI

Just a short story about my father and his uncanny ability to recognize when I was in need--

During my doctoral degree at Peabody (many years ago), I really struggled. The degree program was very challenging and I was living by myself in downtown Baltimore with few friends close by. My father must have recognized my loneliness and anxiety because at the end of every phone conversation, he would remind me of the opening two lines from a fable by Jean de La Fontaine called The Father and his Sons. My father and I had a long history with this fable because when I was in 8th grade, I had to memorize the complete fable for my French class. I remember him helping me with the pronunciation and meaning. Then, 20 plus years later, he starts reciting it to me again, reminding me of the importance of hard work and to never give up on a dream.

It goes something like this:

Travaillez, prenez de la peine, c'est le font qui manque le moins. Translated into English--

The Father and his Sons (BookV, Fable 9)
Work hard, nor trouble spare, nor toil,
Labour's more plentiful than soil.
A wealthy farmer, feeling death draw nigh,
Called round his children, and, no witness by,

When I grow up I want to be . . .

"Beware," he said, "of selling the estate
Our fathers left us, purchased with their
sweat;
For hidden treasure's there.
The spot I know not; but with zeal and care
You'll find it out, and make it yours at last.
Plough up the ground as soon as autumn's
past,
And dig and delve nor grudge the daily pain;
And when you've toiled, return and toil
again."
He died. The sons turned up the field;
Incessant was their toil, and when the year
Was ended, large the produce it did yield,
Though ne'er a hidden treasure did appear.
Wise was the father, ere he died, to show
That labour is the mine whence riches flow.

WORDS FROM CECILE NARBONI

"Thank you all for being here, to be part
of this very special day.

You're here, which means you probably
knew my dad. In one or more of the many
phases of his life . . .

The distinguished pilot and military man,
the doctor with the amazing bedside manner...

When God made Daddy, I think we can all agree, he broke the mold.

I can say, without hyperbole, that I had the best father in the world.

Unconditional love, Daddy was my "yes man." He never said "no" to me, no matter what kind of crazy, outlandish ideas I came up with. Even when he probably should have. That was Daddy. He always said he just wanted me to be happy.

And, frankly, he wanted everyone to be happy. He once told me he left a party in downtown San Antonio, having a nice evening, seeing great friends, good food, good drinks, he left feeling wonderful. Until he told me, he saw a stray dog in the street, obviously hungry, not doing so well. And, he told me that it made him sad, and reminded him that there are others out there who are suffering.

That was my dad. He had a great life, a long healthy successful life. But he always wanted the same for others.

Daddy was unassuming. I could always find his car in the doctors' parking lot. Among the Porsches, Cadillacs, and Mercedes, his diesel Volkswagen Golf was easy to spot.

He never judged anyone else for what they had, or what they didn't have, what job they held, where they came from, race, religion, imaginary things that cause such strife in the world even today. Seriously, who cares?

Even though Daddy came nothing close to being a hippie, he was really all about live and let live.

I never saw him get his feathers ruffled by something someone else said; he didn't obsess about the trivial things that bother the rest of us . . .

We would actually do well to take a page from the Book of Gino: Be sweet, don't judge. If you're having a disagreement with someone about something, find a diplomatic way around it. I try to do this; doesn't always work, but following his example, I do try.

I am still a Daddy's girl. And, I refuse to be too sad. I know that may sound weird as I speak at my father's funeral.

Because we should all be so lucky to have had the long, wonderful life, filled with great friends, a successful marriage, travel . . .

I was with him when he passed away peacefully. I will always be grateful for that. Daddy didn't suffer. Remember within the last few months of his death, Daddy was in the United Arab Emirates, in France where he got to see his brother; he was in northern California with me, eating what he told me were the best fruits of his life.

And, he was in Maine, eating lobster with wonderful new friends.

Two weeks ago, when Daddy knew it was the end, he waited for me to get home. Thoughtful as always, I could tell he held on while I made the trip home.

Passing away less than an hour after I walked through the door.

I literally felt his spirit enter my heart right after he took his last breath.

I've been fearing my dad's passing since I was a teenager and I'm telling you, instead I got many wonderful years with him.

We should all be so lucky to have the wonderful life that Gino had . . .

When I grow up I want to be ...

And, in his spirit, I truly wish that for all of you.

I know that's what he wants, too ..."

WORDS FROM JACK SAYLOR, COL. USAF, MC, RET.

"With apologies to Cecile, I am one of those old retired guys.

Today we are here to say goodbye, but also to celebrate the life of an incredible human being.

I won't recount his superb obituary, but I realized that part of it was almost PC. You know, politically correct. Sooo, I thought I might clarify. It said he had a classic French education and I thought holy cow. It took him 18 years to graduate from medical school! Wow. Classic French Education?? Then it said that he defected from the Vichy French forces (Defected! In the night! In the desert!) And joined the Free French Air Force which had no airplanes. Moreover, it said that while stationed in Lebanon he learned he had been selected for pilot training in the US. Family and friends, what really happened is that he had repeatedly been going AWOL, was finally caught, and was in a Lebanese jail when he was picked up and

291

sent packing. Now it's true that he ended up getting his multiengine pilot's license and USAF wings. You know there must be stories there. He was a young French male after all. But by the time he returned to France the war was over, so back to school. Ah, but it is a Classical French education so he entered

Phase 2: As a pilot with a French passport, he got that fateful call from the Hagana Israeli underground asking him to smuggle planes and supplies to the new embargoed provisional state of Israel.

So on to fight for independence. Having established that he does not shrink from the illegal, he became a key part of the Machal - not a routine or easy smuggling task. Later after becoming a Captain in the IDF, flying instructor and a pilot for the Israeli domestic and international air lines, he took off those uniforms —just quit — and returned to medical school.

Phase 3: apparently still restless, he quit school, or never restarted, and went back to the United States and enlisted in the USAF. He had visions of flying in America, so the efficient post- war government think tank made him an enlisted man and an aircraft mechanic. He was, however, a bona fide, US-trained military pilot, so he wore his wings on his mechanic's uniform. During one inspection visit, a senior air force officer was reviewing the men, all at attention, only to walk back and stare at Gino, his grade, and at his wings. Sergeant's stripes - wings. Sergeant's stripes - wings. Finally, he said "

Boy, I don't know what you did, but it must have been a lulu!"

Discharged after his four year enlistment, he returned to Paris apparently with wild oats all planted, for:

Phase 4: He finally finished medical school. Back to the US, an internship, marriage, becoming a US citizen and again joining the United States Air Force. He finally slowed him down. I think a wife and two daughters helped. They, and the cats all took on a career in the Air Force Medical Corps.

Phase 5: I met him in 1966 as I reported for my first day as a resident in internal medicine at Letterman General Hospital in San Francisco, California. I was one of a few Air Force physicians training in an army hospital, but had been told of another one -

an Italian named Gino. He was giving a lecture that very day which he said was about diseases of the "e-so-phay-goose". Luckily I soon found out he meant esophagus and quickly learned that he wasn't Italian, but French. Turns out there are a lot of English words in medicine that come out very differently with a French accent. I will not entertain you with others. I was fascinated by this Frenchman in an USAF uniform looking older than the staff yet studying as one of us 24-25 year-olds. The more I learned of him, the more in awe of him I became. Our wives became good friends, and our families grew. However as all in the military know, we then went our ways - me to Illinois and Gino to Vietnam (turns out the scientific language in Vietnam is French). Yet another war before settling down after a fellowship in medical oncology at M.D. Anderson Cancer Center.

Phase 6: Just think, this is a man who has worn 6 uniforms, been in three air forces and literally participated in the establishment of a country — all before stepping into a world of the care of those afflicted with cancer. There are a thousand stories there.

Throughout all this he proved to be compassionate, honest, and dedicated to his practice, colleagues, patients, family and friends. If this is not enough he decided to take piano lessons as an octogenarian and professed a long time desire to be an orchestral conductor — never realizing, I think, all the masterpieces that he had conducted thus far.

God smiled on us when he put Gino on this world. I truly have never met a man like him, and I don't think I ever will.

God rest your soul."

WORDS FROM YEHEZKEL CAINE, MD.

Rabbi Scheinberg related the following story to us at the funeral service. Later, I contacted Dr. Caine and asked if he would write about meeting Gino so many years ago in Colorado Springs, Colorado. Here is Dr. Caine's accounting from that time in 1978:

"A bit of background. I was a pilot-physician from the Israeli Air Force and sent on an advanced course in aerospace medicine to Brooks AFB. It was 1978 and I was in the USA for my program at Brooks. That was when I first met Rabbi Scheinberg and Judy with their (then) small boys! Whilst at Brooks I had gone on assignment to visit

NORAD, which, as you know so well, was the North American Air Defense Command buried deep in Cheyenne Mountain in Colorado. It was to remind you, at the height of the cold war so security was very tight. There was I, a young Captain from the Israeli Air Force, visiting one of the most closely guarded and secret installations of the US, the headquarters of the strategic defense of the USA. Needless to say I had someone accompanying me every step of the way. Entry into the command post, deep under the mountain, was by a small electric bus that took us deep into the bowels of the earth. There we entered into a vast cavern where a number of buildings were placed on giant springs - supposedly to help them survive an atomic attack! Into one of these buildings I was led by my escort, an Air Force major if I recall, who, flashing his pass, took me through doors and corridors and into a room. There, sitting behind a desk was a tall, thin – even gaunt – older man, a colonel with pilot's wings.

As I entered he stood to greet me, signaled to the escort to leave (which was very unexpected there, as I was not supposed to go anywhere unescorted), closed the door and then, in a clear voice said to me: "Shalom, baruch haba, shev bevakasha". This, in Hebrew, meant "Shalom, welcome, please sit down".

And then proceeded with another sentence, accented, "Shemi Natan Narboni" which was " my name is Natan Narboni" (at that point he still hadn't used "Gino").

Seeing my surprise (let's face it, the last thing I expected to find half a mile underground in Cheyenne mountain was someone in a USAF uniform speaking Hebrew!) he continued in English (with a mild accent that I couldn't place) and told me his personal story. I was very familiar with the MACHAL, the Hebrew acronym for "volunteers from abroad" and in fact I was very friendly with a few "machalniks" (as they were called affectionately) who had remained in Israel. One, by the name of Jerry Renov had been one of my early flying instructors and another, by the name of Sid Cohen, had also gone on to study medicine and we became friends despite the obvious generational gap (obviously they were much older than me – I was born at the beginning of 1949). Both had been pilots trained in WW2, had flown in various theatres and then, during the War of Independence had volunteered to fly for the fledgling Israeli Air Force. So, here I was, face-to-face with another "genuine" machalnik. In this case, Natan (or to use his nickname – Gino – as he subsequently told me) had continued to fly in Israel after the war as one of the early pilots for El Al before returning to Europe to study medicine and then on to the USA where he became an American and joined the air force. He had not forgotten his time in Israel (which was, at the time just 30 years previously, closer to us then than this event was to us now), and, as mentioned, still remembered some basic Hebrew. We sat there for a long time, he telling me his personal story and, of course, "swapping" war stories, as all "old soldiers" do! He was interested to hear about some of his old friends from the days of MACHAL as he had lost track of most of them since then (it was well before the days of emails and Facebook!). I was mesmerized by the stories that he told of flying during the war of Independence and the early days of the Israeli

Air Force as well as the early days of El Al. He wanted to hear about the Israeli Air Force "today" (that is in 1978!) as well as stories of the Yom Kippur war and the other wars that were not uncommon to the Middle East then (nor now!). We sat there for hours – I think... – and then he took me on a tour of the installation that I doubt if many have had! When time came to leave I think that the escort was totally flummoxed with where I had disappeared to all this time and was probably quite worried!!

Over 4000 volunteers came to fight for Israel during the War of Independence. Some were very well known, with the most famous probably being Gen. Mickey Marcus, who was tragically killed by friendly fire next to the Castel, on the road to Jerusalem. A small group, numbering probably no more than a couple of hundred, came with experience with aircraft - ranging from pilots and other aircrew (such as navigators, radio operators etc.) through mechanics and operations officers. They formed the nucleus of the nascent air force. Israel at the time had essentially no fully trained air force pilots, with just a handful of local boys who had been in the RAF. Without volunteers like Gino there would not have been an Israel Air Force during the war and, almost undoubtedly, the whole outcome of the war would have been dramatically different. At the time the Air Force ran officially in English! The few who served really saved the day and it could well have been to these brave volunteers - many of whom were not even Jewish - that Churchill's immortal words might have been aimed "never, in the field of human conflict, has so much been owed by so many to so few".

Unfortunately, I never had an opportunity to run into Gino again after that. I returned frequently (and still do) to the States but I assume that he was discharged sometime after our meeting and returned to civilian life, so our paths never crossed.

But, that, for me, was a very special and memorable meeting, which even more than 37 years later has remained firmly in a "recess" in my memory, only to be brought to the surface by Rabbi Scheinberg's phone call.

GINO NARBONI
CITATIONS, AWARDS, MEDALS

Certificate of Naturalization
United States of America
9 November 1954

Reciprocal Engine Mechanic Course
March 1955

Aircraft Maintenance Officer Course
7 August 1957

National Defense Service Medal
Good Conduct Medal
1957—Rhein Main Air Base, Germany

Honorable Discharge from the Armed Forces of the United
States Air Force
20 May 1958

Primary Course Aerospace Medicine
September 1962

Bronze Star Medal
National Defense Service Medal
Vietnamese Service Medal with 4 Oak Leaf Clusters
Air Force Outstanding Unit Award with 2 Oak Leaf Clusters
Republic of Vietnam Gallantry Cross
Republic of Vietnam Campaign Medal
Air Force Longevity Service Ribbon with 4 Oak Leaf Clusters
1 October 1968- 1 October 1969

(continued)

Air War College Seminar Program
Maxwell Air Force Base, AL
Graduate
8 July 1973

Meritorious Service Medal
1st Oak Leaf Cluster
1 July 1975-22 July 1977

Meritorious Service Medal, with 2 Oak Leaf Clusters
Air Force Commendation Medal
Chief Flight Surgeon, USAF
31 May 1981

Retirement, Active Duty,
United States Air Force,
1 August 1981

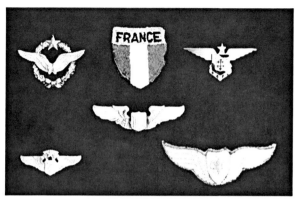

Left, top row
Les ailes de pilote de
l'armée de l'air fran-
çaise
Pilot wings, French Air
Force

The motto of the
French Air Force

L'étoile te guide,
Les ailes te portent,
La couronne de lauriers
t'attend.

The star guides you,
The wings carry you,
The crown of laurels
awaits you.

Center, top row
Official patch worn on
my French uniform
during US Flight
School Training

Right, top row
FAFL
Forces Aerienne, Fran
çaises Libre
Free French Air Forces

Insignia given to me at
Kairouan, Tunisia, after
volunteering and join
ing FAFL.

Center
US Army Air Force
pilot wings
Received at graduation
from Turner Air Base,
Albany, GA.

Left, bottom row
USAF Chief Flight
Surgeon wings
750 logged flying hours

Right, bottom row
Israeli Air Force pilot
wings
Captain, Israeli Air
Force

SCRAPBOOK

....

To my family & friends,

Here are some *souvenirs du temps passé* from my life. The photographs, those from the distant past and those that were recorded more recently, help my journey stay alive in my mind.

I invite you to put faces to the stories.

Marcy Maloy, Photographer

Zihuatanejo, Mexico, 2008

My father's medical school class, University of Paris Medical School, Georges Narboni-seated on windowsill, 1912.

Georges Narboni Captain French Army Medals include: Legion d'Honneur pour faits de guerre, Croix de Guerre with 1 palm, 3 stars

When I grow up I want to be . . .

French-made automobile: Hotchkiss, circa 1930, in Luchon, France. This town
in the Pyrenées is known for its thermal spas. Each year we went to this
station so my father could inhale the vapors from sulfur springs as a treatment
for his chronic lung problems.
*Standing, my cousin Claude Narboni. Seated (left to right) Yvan, my cousin Nicole
Narboni, Mario, and me*

Our house in Sidi Mabrouk, Constantine, Algeria

307

In Sandals (left to right) Yvan, Mario, and Gino

My mother, Aurette Narboni, during her sanitarium stay, 1936

When I grow up I want to be . . .

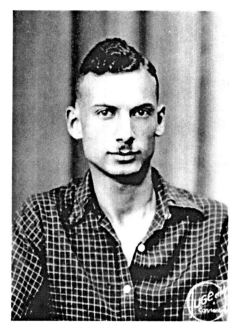

Prior to taking my Bac exam in Constantine. My father made me shave my goatee because he felt the examiner would object to my appearance.

Yvan in Zouave uniform

The getaway truck that took us deserters from Algiers, Algeria to Kairouan, Tunisia

Rayak Air Base, casually dressed, I'm on the right in my underwear

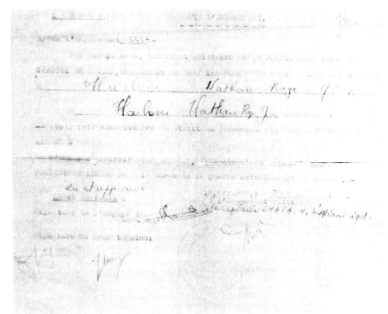

Orders for my induction into Forces Françaises Libre, Free French Forces, 23 May, 1943

November 14, 1944—My first solo flight; Hawthorne School of Aeronautics, Orangeburg, South Carolina. Standing in front of PT-17 airplane. Following tradition, I could now wear my goggles facing forward. Prior to solo flight, the pilot trainee wore the goggles reversed on the back of his head.

Short-snorter: This dollar bill confirms the date of my first solo flight, signed by my instructor. It is still in my wallet, 69 years later.

Staff Sergeant Gino Narboni, Rhein Main Air Base, 1955

Intern, Deaconess Hospital Buffalo, New York, 1961

My mother Aurette and me, Italian holiday, 1956.

When I grow up I want to be . . .

Charlotte and me in Las Vegas, 1964

Lucien Daninos, my uncle, a tenor at the Opéra Comique, circa 1936

313

Official USAF Photo, 1980

With Julia Child in Santa Barbara, 2001
(Left to right) Cecile, Mrs. Child, Charlotte & Gino

Nicole and Cecile buying bread in France. Green Mercedes in rear, 1972.

Nicole Narboni, receiving her DMA (Doctor of Musical Arts) degree, Johns Hopkins University Peabody Institute, May 1992.

Nicole, Charlotte, Gino, Cecile—2003, New York City

315

Cecile and dorado – off the coast of Mexico

In my conducting mode

Suzanne Pack, Photographer

Charlotte's couscous . . . as good as my mother made. Charlotte's assistant, Batman, is taking a break from his labors.

The Narboni Family 2013.
Left to Right: Nicole, Cecile, Gino and Charlotte

When I grow up I want to be . . .

Photo shoot, out-of-town guests seated on the banks of the San Antonio River, Sunday, 17 November 2013.

Monday morning barge ride for out-of-town guests, final day activities for the birthday celebration, 18 November 2013.

When I grow up I want to be . . .

Charlotte and Gino getting ready for the music; Nicole's recital in her father's
honor, 18 November 2013, Steinway Hall, San Antonio, Texas.

Nicole plays Happy Birthday for her father at the conclusion of the recital.

A gift of love from Nicole to her father through music.

Let's have cake and champagne!

When I grow up I want to be ...

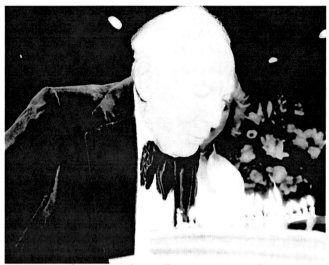

Blowing out the candles at Steinway Hall.

And, a grand time was had by all ... friends at the farewell photo session,
following couscous dinner, 18 November 2013.

Gino answering questions following Jewish Film Festival screening of *Above and Beyond*.

Gino, greeting guests at *When I Grow Up* book signing following the San Antonio Jewish Film Festival, February 2015.

When I grow up I want to be . . .

Aboard Qantas, Airbus A380 Flight, non-stop, Dallas, Texas-Sydney, Australia;
December 2014.

Gino and the captain, Qantas A380. Nothing better than being in a cockpit!

I do, I do

We do,
We did, and
We will do it again...

Please join
Captain Mark Dexter,
Master, Seabourn Odyssey
As he leads us in renewing our marriage vows
On the occasion of our Fifty-Second Wedding Anniversary

Charlotte and Gino Narboni
Thursday, December 18th, 2014
6:30 pm
Suite 700

RSVP Guest Services by dialing 9

This photo was taken for another occasion, but it seemed perfect for the invitation to the ceremony aboard the Seabourn *Odyssey*.

Mark Dexter, Master Seabourn *Odyssey*, as we renew our vows.

The photos in this picture are rendered completely in chocolate, a gift from
the pastry chef, Oberoi Hotel, Dubai, UAE, May 2016

Tel Nof Air Base, with IDF fighter pilots, 2015.

Gino was always happy around planes; the age didn't matter. Restored PT-17,
Collection of Doc Hecker, Bulverde, Texas, 2015.

When I grow up I want to be . . .

Aboard Emirates A380 flight-non-stop Houston to Dubai, May 2016. Charlotte Narboni, All decked out, ready to serve and to taste the Dom Perignon, 2006.

Gino and I, aboard Seabourn *Sojourn*, on our way to Petra, Jordan, with our Aussie friends, Rob Guillemot and John Green. Yes, we're planning another party.

Gino with his favorite food groups: chocolate, cheese, something fried, and any other salty or sweet tidbit.

Gino relaxes on the terrace of the Hotel Raphael, Paris, France on the same balcony where Cary Grant was once photographed. The Arc de Triomphe is in the background on a beautiful day in May, 2016.

When I grow up I want to be . . .

A few of his favorite things: L-R, top-bottom; pommes frites, baklava, chocolates, croissants, French cheeses, fresh California figs. Served at the collation following Gino's funeral, 29 July 2016.

Honor guard, United States Air Force, awaiting final salute to Gino Narboni,
Ft. Sam Houston National Cemetery, San Antonio, Texas, 29 July 2016.

Marker for Gino's grave: Name, rank, military branch, date of birth, date of
death, war service (Vietnam) and medals. Final note: *Il a replié ses ailes.*"
"He has folded his wings."

The family at home following Gino's funeral. Left-right: Shaina Markulin (niece), Charlotte, Cecile, Heath Cole (son-in-law) and Nicole.

RESOURCES

As memories fade with time, we wanted to confirm, as much as possible, our concept of the historical events that helped shape this story. We do not claim to be scholars or historians and any errors are ours alone. The following resources were instrumental in providing information:

- APNFA - Association du Personnel Navigant Formé en Amèrique (Armée de l'Air, Aéronavale)
- CFPNA - Photos Officielles, 14eme Detachment, Les Centres De Formation Du Personnel Navigant En Amèrique C.F.P.N.A 1943-1946
- World Machal - Volunteers from overseas in the Israeli Defense Forces www.machal.org.il Aliyah Bet & Machal Virtual Museum - History of Air Force
- Country Studies.us/Lebanon) - World War II and Independence (published by Library of Congress)
- Jewish Virtual Library - A Project of the American-Israeli Cooperative Enterprise
- About.com - military history, Operation Torch, World War II Operation Torch Invasion of North Africa
- New York Times – Obituary of Jean Pierre-Bloch
- Answers.com - USS *Mariposa* troop carrier
- www.connections.com - Richard Horrell

LIST OF CONTRIBUTORS

Marcy Maloy
Zihuatanejo Photograph, Family Photograph
Back Cover Photograph

Roger and Peggy Thompson Minuteman Press
Printing

Suzanne Pack
Formatting/Editing and Couscous Photograph

The Wood Agency
Cover Design

It is inadequate to simply list the names of those professionals who helped us bring this memoir to life. In this edition, we want to inform our readers that the creative and stylistic work of this book, from the cover, the photographs, the formatting and the printing, is an essential component of its success

We have worked with Marcy Maloy, Skip Wood, and Roger and Peggy Thompson for 25 years. Suzanne Pack is a relative newcomer to this group, but she, like the others, is part of the team. We wouldn't dream of embarking on any project without their counsel.

337

CPSIA information can be obtained
at www.ICGtesting.com
Printed in the USA
FFOW03n0524080418
46157056-47331FF